101 WAYS TO AVOID REINCARNATION

REINCARNATION

or GETTING IT RIGHT THE FIRST TIME

BY HESTER MUNDIS

ILLUSTRATIONS BY PETER SPACEK

WORKMAN PUBLISHING, NEW YORK

For Shirley and Joan; Sally and Peter; Sue and Jill;
Jerry and Richard; Malcolm and Marco.

And Ron, of course, who taught me
the Tao of everything.

Library of Congress Cataloging-in-Publication Data

Mundis, Hester.
    101 ways to avoid reincarnation, or, Getting it right the first time.

    1. New Age movement—Humor.   I. Title.   II. Title:
One hundred one ways to avoid reincarnation.
PN6231.N556M8   1989   818'.5402   88-40606
ISBN 0-89480-383-2

Back cover photograph by Walt Chrynwski
Cover and book design by Charles Kreloff

Workman Publishing
708 Broadway
New York, New York 10003

Printed in the United States of America

First printing October 1989

10 9 8 7 6 5 4 3 2 1

CONTENTS

INTRODUCTION

THERE'S NO TIME like the present to start thinking about tomorrow, which is why I've written this guide to enlightenment now.

After an amazing journey of self-discovery that began with an epiphany in Bloomingdale's and took me beyond the limits of rational experience, maxed out my credit cards, and became a whirlwind intensive in heightened consciousness that makes Shirley Mac-Laine's look like a stroll through the mall, I've discovered that reincarnation is not a birthright. It's more a birth wrong. In fact, it's "flunking life" and having to take it over and over again until you get it right and can dwell eternally in blissful omniscience and astral retirement. Getting it right the first time through enlightenment is what this book is all about.

In it you will find—distilled, demystified, and reduced to its lowest cosmic denominator—the essence of the New Age movement. It doesn't matter if you're just curious whether you've ever lived before, merely confused about crystals, or simply wish you could talk to yourself and mean it, everything you ever wanted to know about unfoldment but didn't want to attend a New Age workshop to find out is here.

It is my sincerest hope that you consider this book a valuable tool, an owner's manual for your afterlife, an addition to your library. It is meant to be read, studied, shared—but never, never to be given to a friend who has enough money to buy his or her own copy!

1

WHAT'S YOUR NEW AGE POTENTIAL?

THE NEW AGE is a loose mixture of ancient mythologies, modern science and Eastern religions that defies precise definition. Nonetheless, it is dedicated to increasing personal and planetary awareness (see Chapter 5, "Put On Your Brights"), which is absolutely essential for avoiding life-flunking and unwanted incarnations.

The quiz that follows has been designed specifically to provide a fair evaluation of your intrinsic New Age knowledge as well as to give you a pretty good idea of your New Age potential and chances of getting life right the first time.

Answer the following questions as best you can without consulting Jeane Dixon, Dear Abby, or anyone who's been dead for over 5,000 years.

1. You think of life as . . .
   a) a grind
   b) a magazine
   c) a learning experience

2. You think of death as . . .
   a) painful
   b) final
   c) a new beginning

3. You believe that chakras are . . .
   a) candy bars
   b) Oriental women's breasts
   c) important for body and soul togetherness

4. You think a high colonic is . . .
   a) the Eiffel Tower
   b) a tall shaman
   c) inspirational irrigation and a good time

5. You think ESP is . . .
   a) something women have before their periods
   b) a high-performance motor oil
   c) a natural potentiality

6. You believe that Lazarus is . . .
   a) someone raised from the dead by Jesus
   b) a 100% pure bioactive vegetable mouthwash
   c) a channeled entity who talks funny

7. You think the right brain is . . .
   a) correct
   b) creative
   c) not in *your* head

8. You think the left brain is . . .
   a) logical
   b) liberal
   c) not always right

9. You think yin and yang . . .
   a) can't mate in captivity
   b) are Chinese traffic signals
   c) are made for each other

10. You feel that cigarettes are . . .
    a) a nasty habit
    b) carcinogenic
    c) okay if sansemilla

11. You think the astral plane is . . .
    a) faster than the *Concorde*
    b) an outer-space woodworking tool
    c) a soul-service rest area

12. You thank people for sharing . . .
    a) their seats
    b) beach houses
    c) detailed descriptions of intimate bodily functions

13. You think an out-of-body experience is . . .
    a) having a baby
    b) faking an orgasm
    c) better than the Bahamas

14. You think a mantra is . . .
    a) a giant insect
    b) a Korean car
    c) a sacred chant

15. You would be most upset if you were . . .
    a) out of money
    b) out of luck
    c) out of herbal tea

16. You believe that essential oils are . . .
    a) ingredients in shampoo
    b) low in cholesterol
    c) psychically uplifting

17. You think channeling is . . .
    a) switching TV stations
    b) swimming from France to England
    c) a rewarding dead entity job

18. You think Machu Picchu is . . .
    a) a famous French mime
    b) a spicy Pakistani rice dish
    c) a Peruvian global power point

How did you score?

If you answered c) to all or most of the questions: Your New Age potential is undeniable. You're not only ready to learn how to avoid reincarnation, you're willing and able to die right now.

If you didn't answer c) to all or most of the questions: Your New Age potential is a cosmic joke. Don't worry about reincarnating—nobody even knows you're alive!

▲

2

ASTRAL PLANE RESERVATIONS

MOST FLUNKING AT LIFE is caused by inadequate knowledge of death. The astral plane, for instance, where your soul goes when you do, is frequently confused with the space shuttle or dismissed as nonexistent. But just because it doesn't appear on any maps, there are no pictures of it and most of its inhabitants are dead is no reason to rush to misjudgment. Aside from being the broadcast station for all messages from beyond and the home of Shirley MacLaine's personal spirit guides, this place is the Riviera of the afterlife, the Club Med of the cosmos, so any reservations you may have about believing in—or hanging out on—the astral plane should be canceled immediately.

There's no earthly reason why any enlightened bodiless spirit would want to leave this celestial spa. The advantages of permanent, eternal residence are all stress-free and out of this world.

You never have to worry about:

- What to wear
- Setting the VCR
- Flossing after meals
- Safe sex
- Putting your foot in your mouth
- Where something has been before

- Shaving your legs
- Which fork to use
- Ring around the collar
- The weather
- Running out of toilet paper
- Losing your hair
  or, of course,
- dying.

3

KARMA, KARMA, KARMA CHAMELEONS

IF THERE IS ANY New Age tenet you absolutely *must* understand, it's karma: *the* basic cosmic law of cause and effect, which holds that every deed, good or bad, receives due retribution. What you sow is what you reap. And if you're not a good sower, you're going to weep more than reap in this life and the next, and the next, until you get it right and can finally quit sowing and relax on the astral plane as an enlightened spirit entity forevermore. That this is essential for achieving release from endless rounds of birth and death cannot be stressed strongly enough. And it isn't. Karma is still the number one cause of reincarnation in the world—and people *continue* to bring it on themselves!

This is due largely to a lack of karman knowledge. For instance, not everyone knows there are three types of karma (and that's not counting good and bad). Then again, not everyone cares.

The Three Karmas

BOOMERANG KARMA: A harmful action toward another comes back to the perpetrator, eye for eye, tooth for tooth, in this life or succeeding ones.

Example: If you were a thief in 12th-century Baghdad, expect to be robbed in 20th-century Brooklyn.

ORGANISMIC KARMA: What you did to excess with your body in a former life will be denied to you in this one.

Example: If you were a charter member at Roman orgies, you'll soon be as sexually active as a eunuch.

SYMBOLIC KARMA: Metaphorical version of Boomerang Karma.

Example: If you ever took scalps as trophies, your dome is doomed to be balder than a baby's bottom.

4

Determining the Sex of Your Parents

Because new age philosophy also holds that we create our own realities and choose our own parents so we can work out past conflicts with karma-compatible folks, it is important for avoiding reincarnation (to say nothing of serious problems in this and future lifetimes) to determine their sex as soon as possible.

The one with the penis is your father. The one without the penis is your mother.

5

Put On Your Brights: Achieving Awareness

Insufficient enlightenment is the most common cause of poor inner vision and concomitant reincarnations. If you can't see that you're a deserving human being, that you're part of the planet, part of the whole wondrous oneness of everything, *put on your brights!*

Awareness is a basic prerequisite for living as well as for realizing your optimal personal and planetary potential. So, don't wait. Get with it! Just remember one thing: awareness isn't achieved in a day—*but it shouldn't take you a lifetime, either!*

6

AFFIRMATIVE-PLUS AFFIRMATIONS

(For Those Heavy Days When Nothing Seems Right)

ONE OF THE MOST effective ways to make Karma-corrective changes in *this* lifetime is to use strong positive thoughts—called "affirmations"—to replace whatever negative beliefs have taken root in your subconscious.

For overriding light negative beliefs, such as "I'm a terrible bridge player" or "I can't possibly accept this expensive gift," ordinary affirmations such as "I am a wonderful person" and "I deserve the best" are fine. But to counteract heavily ingrained negatives, you'll find that affirmative-plus affirmations are the way to go.

Here are some examples:

Heavy negative: "I'm so dumb—I have to study for my blood tests."

Affirmative-plus affirmation: "I'm so smart—my answering machine asks me questions."

Heavy negative: "I'm so fat—I could donate my body to four different medical schools."

▲

Affirmative-plus affirmation: "I'm so gorgeous—Fotomat pays me for my snapshots."

Heavy negative: "I'm such a coward—I'm afraid to cross a *T*."

Affirmative-plus affirmation: "I'm so brave—I'd wear live alligator shoes."

Heavy negative: "I'm such a klutz—I can't say 'hello' without spilling my guts."

Affirmative-plus affirmation: "I'm so careful—I never even drop a name."

7

CREATIVE VISUALIZATIONS FOR ALL OCCASIONS

THE NEW AGE THEORY of creative visualization is *What you see is what you get*. And it works, more or less. I mean, you might visualize yourself behind the wheel of a brand-new Porsche convertible and find yourself six months later driving your brother-in-law's second-hand Pinto—but, hey, that's not shabby for half a year of daydreaming. And daydreaming is basically all that visualization is.

The reason most people have problems in their lives, have had problems in past lives and will continue to have problems in future lives is *astigmatic visualization*. This is a defect in positive focusing, manifested by closing the eyes and imagining the worst (e.g., getting seasick on a cruise, getting on the wrong plane, getting trapped in an elevator with a monkey corpse). But this defect is curable!

All you have to do is relax in the privacy of your own inner space and see yourself *already enjoying* whatever it is you want in your life. You must remember, though, to think *only in the present tense* and to be

▲

specific. The universe is infinite in its goodness, but don't expect it to read your mind!

Specifically Creative Visualizations

To increase VISA credit:
<u>See</u> *yourself blithely purchasing vintage wines in assorted flavors.*

To achieve multiple orgasms:
<u>See</u> *yourself engaged in nonstop passionate sex with twins—and smoking cigarette after cigarette.*

To get backstage passes to rock concerts:
<u>See</u> *yourself emerging from a limo and walking confidently through the crowd with Mick Jagger or Princess Diana.*

To get a promotion:
<u>See</u> *yourself sitting in a corner office with lots of windows, fondling a paycheck with lots of zeros.*

To look 10 years younger:
<u>See</u> *yourself gazing into the eyes of a board-certified plastic surgeon—and forking over the paycheck that came with your promotion.*

8

DECORATING YOUR OWN INNER SPACE*

WHETHER YOU'RE INTO French provincial, Tibetan contemporary or Peruvian flake, the New Age rule for decorating your own inner space is *no clutter*! This is not only because you need room to let in enlightenment, but also because whatever you choose you're going to have to live with for a long, long time.

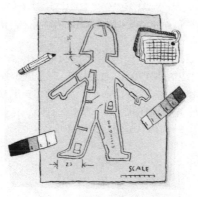

---

*in'ner space   *n.* the space within you that you are never without.

9
HOLISTIC HOUSEKEEPING

HOLISTIC AND NEW AGE go together like love and marriage, horse and carriage—you can't have one without the other, and you certainly can't avoid life-flunking if you think otherwise! Holism and *wholeism*. Holistic housekeeping, therefore, requires seeing housework not as a series of diverse domestic chores, but for what it really is: *one big burden.*

Homes are more than just combinations of floors, walls, doors and windows. They're scratched furniture, spotted carpets, stained sinks, smelly toilets, ringed bathtubs, soiled laundry, messy closets, dirty dishes, finger-smudged major appliances and little dust-catching knickknacks. If you ignore any of these, your living space will always lack *whole* cleanliness and never look as good as your neighbor's.

As our bodies are temples for our souls, so our homes are temples for our bodies, and simply dusting off an altar today and polishing a chalice tomorrow is no way to treat a temple. If you're going to do a job, do the *whole* job—or cough up the dough for someone who will before it's too late!

10

THE NECESSARY "NESS" WORDS

OF PRIMARY IMPORTANCE in deploying your full creative and metaphysical powers, not to mention bonding on contact with other New Agers (at least this time around), is the extensive and excessive verbal and written use of the suffix "ness." The reason for this is obscure, but four out of five transcendentalists agree that "ness" (though not an actual mantra or sacred incantation) is as integral to higher consciousness and enlightenment as MDs are to doctors, CBs are to truckers, and CDs are to yuppies.

Because virtually all words can be suffixed with "ness," and because not all "nesses" are appropriately New Age (Eliot, for instance), you should familiarize yourself with those that are the most positive and popular—and use them as frequently as possible.

The Top 30 New Age "Ness" Words

- Specialness
- Wholeness
- Oneness
- Beingness
- Isness
- Unlimitedness
- Positiveness
- Forgiveness
- Wellness
- Willingness

- Completeness
- Spiritualness
- Wonderfulness
- Perfectness
- Creativeness
- Peacefulness
- Incredibleness
- Consciousness

- Happiness
- Goodness
- Cleanliness
- Kindness
- Givingness
- Lovingness
- Graciousness
- Godliness

with the personal connectives
- Youness, Meness, Usness
and Weness

Caution: Use of more than three of the above "ness" words in a single sentence can be dangerous to diabetics.

11

How to Talk to Yourself and Mean It

WILLINGNESS, BEINGNESS and isness aside, people have a tendency to say things to themselves that they don't really mean (a major cause of flunking at life). For instance, when you forget to do something, you might say to yourself: "Boy, my mind is a sieve." But you don't really *mean* your mind is a sieve. In fact, you *know* it isn't because you wouldn't have remembered that you'd forgotten something if it were.

Learning to talk to yourself and *mean* it, therefore, is not only important for spiritual health but imperative for achieving your full human potential. And, believe it or not, it's as easily said as done.

All you have to do is preface whatever positive statement you make to yourself—"I am God's gift to women/men," "I am entitled to have my cake and eat it, too," "I am perfect, therefore I think I am perfect"—with one of the following four empowerment phrases.

Your Personal Empowerment Phrases

"This is the last time I'm going to say this to me!"
"I'm telling me this once and for all!"
"I don't want to have to say this to me again!"
"Read my lips!"

▲

12

SENDING POSITIVE MESSAGES

NEGATIVITY BEGETS negativity. Additionally, aside from stunting personal growth and being highly conducive to repetitive reincarnations, it can make your life a living hell.

If you want positive results, you must send out positive messages. It doesn't matter whether they're to the universe, your unconscious, your boss, your ex, an answering machine or the milkman, as long as they're positive. For example, if you want to dump your current lover, a positive empowerment message such as "I embrace all wonderful human beings and shall surround myself with only beautifulness from this day forth" will do more to improve your karma than "I hate you, pig, and I never want to see your disgusting face again!"

Here are some other comparisons to help you get the hang of it:

POSITIVE MESSAGE	NEGATIVE MESSAGE
"My body will be transported freely and effortlessly whenever I wish it to be."	*"I'm not going to pay a lot for this muffler!"*

▲

Positive Message	Negative Message
"I enjoy the sounds of silence."	*"I don't have to listen to this noise."*
"I am filled to overflowing with the goodness of the universe and blessed with enough calcium to save infinite numbers of God's creatures from osteoporosis. Thank you."	*"No milk today."*
"I choose to sleep in heavenly peace."	*"Not tonight, I have a headache."*
"I am free to do things as I wish."	*"No way, José."*
"Be happy."	*"Don't worry."*

13

ENTERTAINING NEGATIVES AND OTHER NEW AGE GAFFES

ASIDE FROM INTERFERING with personal and planetary harmony, negativity in any form is socially and spiritually gauche. Anyone who says "I may or may not be right" is entertaining a negative and deserves a slap on the psyche. If you can't say something positive, don't say it at all! (The universe *is*—not "might be.")

Other New Age gaffes that you want to watch out for, not only to avoid reincarnation but to avoid stoning, are:

- Surfing on oil spills
- Taking prescription drugs in public
- Removing the catalytic converter from your car— and boasting about it
- Using pesticides as air fresheners
- Asking for an ashtray
- Referring to sprouts as "bean sperm"
- Taking up taxidermy
- Refusing tofu
- Owning a fly swatter
- Calling Indians "Indians"

▲

14

RESISTING YOUR RESISTANCE TO CHANGE

YOU CAN'T AVOID reincarnation by staying the way you are, yet most of us have a problem with change. Particularly *small change*. Since most metaphysical counselors agree that all our adult values are based on what we believed about ourselves and life when we were kids, this resistance may have stemmed from hearing such negative phrases as:

"Here's a nickel—get lost."

"For two cents I'd punch you in the nose."

"A penny for your thoughts."

"Who asked for your two cents?"

"Ideas like yours are a dime a dozen."

Because of such negative early conditioning, most people regularly toss whatever change they have in their pockets or purses at day's end into a drawer or jar and forget about it, only to find themselves annoyed and frustrated the following day when they have to break a dollar to come up with, say, 13 cents sales tax or a quarter for the phone.

To eliminate these repetitive patterns of childish resistance to change, sit down this instant and make a list of all the uses for change that you can think of— *and then write it over again 100 times!*

15

PROSPERITY CONSCIOUSNESS

LIKE CHANGE, money is an essential New Age tool (see Chapter 67, "Healing with Money"), and understanding the principles and techniques of its use is unquestionably important for making decisions that will have great global and personal impact in the future. But there's absolutely no need to spend hundreds of dollars and valuable time going to workshops on prosperity consciousness. If you're *alive*, you're conscious of prosperity!

Wake up and smell that Morning Thunder! It's very simple: either you have money or you don't. If you're not sure whether you have *enough* money, don't put a down payment on any bridges until you've read the following.

You DO have enough money if:

- You're driven to and from your office in an automobile equipped with a TV, VCR and hot tub.
- You water your plants with Perrier.
- There are solid-gold faucets in your bathroom.
- You go to Tokyo for sushi.
- Your last name is Mellon, Forbes or Trump.
- You've never seen a coin-operated washing machine.
- Your kid's building blocks are Fifth and Madison avenues.
- You buy Dom Pérignon in six-packs.

You DON'T have enough money if:

- Refundable bottles are your primary source of income.
- You think "gourmet dinner" means microwavable.
- Name-brand paper towels are a luxury.
- Your kids' only toys are their toes.
- "Dining out" means eating on your porch.
- You share a toothbrush.
- "Convenience foods" are anything you find in the trash.
- The only ground transportation you can afford is your feet.
- There are more than five people sleeping in your bed.

16

HOW TO PLAY A CONVERGENCE ON YOUR HARMONICA

IF THE PAST 5,000 or so years haven't been your best, take heart! According to the Mayan calendar (regrettably, not widely distributed at Christmas time by gas stations and liquor stores), the earth will be passing out of this dubiously "great" cycle and entering a cosmically terrific "synchronization phase" (where I'll be OK, you'll be OK, and so will everything else) in less than three decades.* That's 2012 for those who want to make New Year's party plans early—and plenty of time to learn how to play a convergence on a harmonica.

All you need to achieve the proper vibrational toning needed for a harmonica convergence is a mouth organ and a dream, ideally one of global harmony (though any involving reforestation of the Amazon basin, whales' rights, Quetzalcoatl or your higher self will work). Then, get together with some friends, hold hands, and with a big smile on your face put the harmonica to your lips and *hum*—or *ho-hum*—for seven minutes. This might seem like a long time—*but not if you keep in mind that you only have to do it once every 23,412 years!*

---

*Thanks to Jose Argüélles, father of the Harmonic Convergence, who convinced 144,000 New Agers around the world to hold hands and hum on August 16 and 17 in 1987 to forestall Armageddon, we are assured of this.

17

NEW AGE MUSIC YOU CAN SING

NOTHING SOOTHES the body, mind and spirit like the mellow, visionary sounds of New Age music. Some of it is so relaxing, in fact, that the labels include warnings against listening to it while driving or using heavy-duty laundry detergents.

Although it's true that for centuries music has been acknowledged as having calming, healing powers, and that its universal energies have been used by prophets and for profits by mystics and moviemakers alike, New Age music is essentially Novocain on a sound track. Songs featuring loons at dusk, herons flapping in flight, plants vibrating and water trickling over rocks—backed up by Celtic harps, Tibeten chimes, biwas, bonangs, bucinas and digitally synthesized tam-tams—just aren't ones most people leave the hot tub humming.

But don't be frustrated if this music isn't your cup of rose hips. There are plenty of classic songs that share the same peace-love-wholeness-oneness-environmentally harmonious spirit and values. And not only can you enjoy those that follow without fear of coma—*but you can actually sing them!*

Sing-Along New Age Classics

- "Accentuate the Positive"
- "After You're Gone"
- "Ah, Sweet Mystery of Life"
- "All You Need Is Love"
- "The Best Things in Life Are Free"
- "Beyond the Blue Horizon"
- "Body and Soul"
- "The Breeze and I"
- "Catch a Falling Star"
- "Climb Every Mountain"
- "Dear Hearts and Gentle People"
- "Did You Ever See a Dream Walking?"
- "Don't Worry, Be Happy"
- "Dream Weaver"
- "Everything's Coming Up Roses"
- "Feelings"
- "Ghost Riders in the Sky"
- "I Believe"
- "I Talk to the Trees"
- "I'll Be Seeing You"
- "I'm Forever Blowing Bubbles"
- "I'm Gonna Sit Right Down and Write Myself a Letter"
- "I've Got a Rainbow Round My Shoulder"
- "I've Told Every Little Star"
- "Keep Your Sunny Side Up"
- "Let a Smile Be Your Umbrella"
- "Let's All Sing Like the Birdies Sing"
- "Life Is Just a Bowl of Cherries"
- "Moonlight Becomes You"
- "More than You Know"
- "My Heart Stood Still"
- "My Time Is Your Time"
- "On a Clear Day You Can See Forever"
- "Over the Rainbow"

- "*Que Serà, Serà*"
- "*Sitting on Top of the World*"
- "*Stairway to Paradise*"
- "*Sunday, Monday, and Always*"
- "*Thanks for the Memory*"
- "*Till the End of Time*"
- "*Till We Meet Again*"
- "*When You Wish upon a Star*"
- "*Where or When*"
- "*With My Eyes Wide Open I'm Dreaming*"
- "*You Are My Lucky Star*"
- "*You Are My Sunshine*"
- "*You'll Never Walk Alone*"

18

MAKING THE RIGHT IMPRESSION ON YOUR HIGHER SELF

YOUR HIGHER SELF is your very best friend, your inner guide to what's right and what's not, your personal 24-hour-a-day adviser on how to succeed at life without ever listening to New Age music. Tuned in to the universal source of all wisdom, the collective unconscious, your higher self knows *everything*—at least everything there is to know.

Even if you don't care about reincarnation, you have to admit that mistrusting your higher self would be just plain stupid. Below are some do's and don'ts on how to keep on its good side.

DO address your higher self in the first person, or the royal "we," whenever making affirmations or asking for guidance.

DON'T ever call your higher self "kiddo."

DO keep a straight face when your higher self says you already have everything you want.

DON'T ask your higher self trick questions.

DO remember to say "please" and "thank you."

DON'T whine or beg.

DO whatever your higher self tells you.

DON'T be a smart-ass.

19

TURNING YOUR INSIGHTS OUT

INSIGHTS COME FROM suddenly recognizing things that your higher self has known all along (your mother is just a grown-up little girl; it takes two to make a pair; carry-all bags never do; enlightenment doesn't strike twice at the same price) and work best for preventing life-flunking if turned out on a daily basis.

As important as this is, it's surprisingly easy. Your higher self has limitless intelligence and will provide answers on a need-to-know basis. Needless to say, though, if you want to avoid reincarnation, you need to know *now*!

20

No-Accident Assurance

FOR EVERY MISHAP we have, every misstep and mistake we make, there is a karmic reason. In the New Age there are no accidents. Although this might be difficult to explain to someone whose car you've just totaled, it's really as simple as that.

We create our own realities for a purpose: to resolve past conflicts, to learn something that will help us finally get life right. This doesn't mean that we always *learn what we ought to*—but nobody said anything about the universe providing no-jerk assurance.

21

WHY GOOD THINGS HAPPEN TO BAD PEOPLE

GOOD THINGS HAPPEN. If they happen to happen to bad people, so what?

Take Countess Elizabeth Bathory. In 1560 she killed more than 50 young girls and used their blood as an all-over body moisturizer. When found out, she received a punishment that was no more severe than being sent to her room. (Admittedly, for life—but it *was* a castle!) How did she luck out? She had "Countess" before her name and Twinkies in her pocket.

Then there was Colonel Thomas Blood. He stole the British crown jewels in 1675 (a capital offense), but instead of being hanged was given a lifetime annual pension by Charles II. How did this come about? Through a hushed-up royal flush of embarrassment.

And then, of course, there was Adolf Hitler. Here was a mean-spirited little housepainter with one testicle who ordered the execution of millions of people, yet became the ruler of one of the most powerful nations on earth, owned more cars than you could park at a mall, innumerable mansions, an underground bunker,

8,960 acres of land in Colorado, and was voted *Time* magazine's Man of the Year.

Go know.

So what if drug dealers have Lear jets and corrupt politicians get pardons? It's none of your business; get on with your own life.

Now, if good things didn't happen to *anyone*, then there would be something to complain about.

22

WHAT YOU'RE REALLY ENTITLED TO

WHAT MAKES the New Age great is its belief that you not only deserve what you get, *you deserve it all!*

You are a worthy, wonderful human being.

The universe loves you.

You are entitled to everything you want.

This is kindergarten-level enlightenment. Unless you have it, or don't rewire your thinking fast, you might as well resign yourself to return engagements as a deprived, embittered loser. If you *do* have it but are uncertain about what you're really entitled to, it would be wise to familiarize yourself with the following.

You are really entitled to:

- Itemized phone bills
- Bank statements
- A jury of your peers
- A choice of beverage
- An equal opportunity employer
- The right to remain silent
- Receipts for purchases
- Bags for your groceries
- Elastic in your underwear

23

WHAT YOU'RE REALLY NOT ENTITLED TO

YES, YOU ARE A WORTHY, wonderful human being.

Yes, the universe loves you.

Still, believe it or not, there are some things you're really *not* entitled to, no matter how worthy you are.

You are really <u>not</u> entitled to:

- Your neighbor's wife (or husband)
- Someone else's seat
- Payola
- Classified information
- An eye for an eye
- A concealed weapon
- A jury of your relatives
- A pirated copy of *E.T.*
- Help at a self-service station

24

SAMPLING NATURE'S RESTAURANT
(or How to Weed-Whack a Salad)

VEGETARIANISM IS chicly New Age. This has something to do with animal flesh containing killer cholesterol and hazardous hormones (increasing the risk of premature departure), but not much. Mostly, it has to do with unequivocally loving and respecting the rights of all our fellow creatures—particularly those that bleed—and therefore not eating them.

Plants, which are also loved and respected, have rights, too, but not as many. This is evidenced by the lack of group protests against farmers who raise innocent vegetables to be sold as food—and by the rising popularity of salad bars among mind, body, and spirit conscious New Agers.

Noted metaphysical counselor Louise L. Hay, author of *You Can Heal Your Life,* considers all plants fair game. As she says in her book, "If it grows, eat it. If it doesn't grow, don't eat it."

With all due respect to Ms. Hay and vegetarians, *not* in *my* book!

If you want to weed-whack a salad (and I admit it's a great way to whip up a meal and trim your lawn at the same time), be sure to check out the weeds you whack. Dandelions may be delightful with dressing, but add some fool's-parsley by mistake and it'll be the last one you make this time around.

My feeling is this: If everything that grew and was green was good for you, only the unenlightened would ever clean out a refrigerator.

25
WE ARE ALL FOOD

WE ARE ALL PARTS of the same whole, a choral interaction of the "I" of one being, both the yin and the yang. We are the world. We are the children. We are the flowers in spring, the birdies that sing, the sunbeams that shine—and we are all food.

So next time you make a salad, toss it gently. Those aren't just leafy greens in a bowl; they're you, they're me, they're *us*!

26

INTUITIVE GARDENING

FORGET ABOUT New Age radionics, which holds that all matter, dead or alive, radiates energy and is therefore part of the planet, part of the cosmos, part of you—in other words, injudiciously pruning a berry bush is like pulling the plug on your mother. Although it's important to realize that plants have feelings and needs, you don't have to drive yourself bonkers catering to them.

Forget about charting the biorhythms of your green beans or buying a CD for your cauliflower. No matter how good these are for your veggies, they're unnecessary for avoiding reincarnation.

If you're a gardener, *trust yourself* and the instructions on seed packets. If something grows, it grows; if it doesn't, try something else. (A little transplantdental meditation always helps.)

Whatever you do, don't feel guilty about pulling up weeds. They're simply plants without re-earthing control. They'll be back.

Your higher self knows what to dig for, so sow your oats where you please—just don't expect them to come up as bran muffins.

27

WORKSHOP ETIQUETTE

NO MATTER WHAT problems you're wrestling with, you can wrest assured because there's a self-help workshop for all of them.

New Age workshops, much like the self-awareness and encounter groups of the '60s, come in a variety of forms and formats—seminars, intensives, retreats, trainings, approaches, practices, experiences, excursions, journeys, adventures, jaunts—but they share the same proprieties. Being unaware of these proprieties is transpersonally gauche, inhibits enlightenment *and can embarrass you to the point where you wish you'd never been born!*

Workshop No-Nos

- Paying registration fees with bad checks
- Cracking gum during meditation
- Smoking cigarettes—especially while doing yoga, T'ai Chi, intensive massage, or rebirthing
- Smoking hams
- Bringing snacks for your compulsive-eating group
- Asking for Sweet 'N Low at a tea ceremony
- Ralphing while Rolfing
- Shaving your legs—during reflexology
- Bringing magnets to a polarity therapy group
- Using a tensor lamp to enhance your aura

- Faking another organism
- Being late for a procrastination group
- Punting while goal-setting
- Eating sushi while swimming with dolphins
- Putting a dimmer switch on your inner light
- Calling women's studies "girl talk"
- Carrying an Uzi

28

SELF-HELP GROUPIES

THERE IS SUCH a plethora of healing, homeopathic, holistic havens of self-help (an oxymoron if there ever was one) that the number of "self-help" groupies is rapidly becoming astronomical. And ridiculous.

With New Age workshops for everything from coping with chronic crab grass and preparing for postpartum wealth to learning to live with junk mail and establishing compassionate relationships with adult children of extraterrestrials, it's a wonder there are still women who can apply lipstick without a workshop support group.

I'm not saying that to get life right you have to pull yourself up by your own bootstraps—*but you ought to at least be able to tie your own shoes!*

29

RECOGNIZING MIRACLES

SOMETHING THAT CAUSES wonder and astonishment, being extraordinary in itself and inexplicable by normal standards, is considered a miracle. That there are people actually paying hundreds of dollars for workshop courses to learn this is itself astonishing, extraordinary and inexplicable.

And totally unnecessary for avoiding reincarnation.

Sure, times change (turning water into wine was once considered a miracle and today it's a California cooler), but there are still plenty of miracles around. And you don't have to be a visionary to recognize them.

Modern-Day Miracles Anyone Can Recognize

- No-wax floors
- Stay-free maxi pads
- Phyllis Diller's face lift
- Self-starting lawn mowers
- Frost-free refrigerators
- No-fault divorce
- Canned laughter
- Faux pearls
- Dry ice
- Odorless garlic
- Richard Nixon's pardon
- Instant soup
- Non-reflecting glass
- Test-tube babies
- Artificial tears
- Meatless hamburgers
- George Burns

30

SOLVING INTERSPECIES COMMUNICATION PROBLEMS

THERE'S MORE TO New Age communication than just being able to contact your higher self or an enlightened spirit entity. You have to learn to communicate with *all* live things on the planet.

That there is an interspecies connection between humans and dolphins, for instance, is now almost universally accepted by New Agers. In fact, swimming with these creatures of alleged superior intelligence in order to learn the secrets of their harmonious sense of community has become one of the hottest—and most expensive—New Age recreations.

But if you're not a swimmer, or are reluctant to shell out $700 for a dip in a fish tank, don't fret. There are plenty of other interspecial pursuits to choose from.

Alternatives to Swimming with Dolphins

Fetching with dogs	Laughing with hyenas
Pecking with chickens	Howling with wolves
Hooting with owls	Honking with geese

Trumpeting with elephants
Dancing with bears
Chirping with birds
Grazing with cows
Slithering with snakes

Buzzing with bees
Gobbling with turkeys
Playing with possum
Cooing with doves
Humping with camels

31

GODDESS WORSHIP

NEW AGE FASCINATION with—and exaltation of—goddesses is widespread, trendy and irrelevant. Unless she's the Universal Mother Isis, the Mother Goddess Shakti, Buffalo Woman or Marilyn Monroe, worshiping a goddess, in private or at a workshop, isn't worth sacrificing your time for.

Not only do such practices decrease chances of avoiding reincarnation and passage of the ERA, but they're blatantly sexist—*and could set the women's movement back a hundred million years!*

32

SOUL PURPOSES

THE MOST OBVIOUS advantage of avoiding reincarnation is freeing that accumulation of energy known as your soul so that it doesn't have to take on another body, particularly after you've spent years getting the one you have into shape. (Imagine never having to watch another Fonda video—ever!)

Unfortunately, the big problem with souls is that they can't be seen *unless* they're wearing a body. Because of this, many people ignore them or treat them as if they didn't exist—*until it's too late.*

The time for achieving soul awareness is *now*! Take a moment and think about this:

Without soul James Brown would sound like Pat Boone.

Without soul Old King Cole would be a merry old despot.

Without soul chitlins would just be the small intestines of swine.

Without soul spiritual counselors would have nothing to save.

Without soul Faust would have had nothing to sell.

Remember: You may have a hundred lifetimes, but you have only one soul—*and a soul is a terrible thing to waste.*

33

THE HAPPY MEDIUM

MEDIUMS (PSYCHICS, CHANNELS, clairvoyants, shamans or other paranormally gifted intermediaries through whom spirits of the dead can contact the living) have the ability to mentally access knowledge that lies beyond conscious awareness. This knowledge can be anything from an afterlife afterthought of a great spiritual leader to a premonition of unannounced advance ticket sales for a Michael Jackson concert, but once imparted it is revered by New Agers as a valuable tool for enlightenment. Although this knowledge is potentially helpful in avoiding reincarnation, no guarantees are given. In any case, a happy medium is one who gets the message—especially since many have likened the experience to doing LSD and getting paid for it.

On the other hand, many mediums are happy simply because they're not a large or an extra-large.

34

CHANNELING FOR DOLLARS

THE NEW AGE phenomenon of channeling enables ordinary people to make large sums of money merely by becoming intermediaries and allowing a deceased personality (or entity) to speak through them about how to get life right through peace, love and oneness. Although this can be annoying, particularly since most channeled entities pontificate in archaic locutions and indefinable accents, it beats working at McDonald's.

It also beats selling insurance, wrapping nails, doing magazine layouts, and washing floors. Jach Pursel, for instance, picked up on this in 1974. A Florida insurance salesman, he was catching some Zs between policies one day when he suddenly began talking in a strange voice about an evolving, spiritually united universe. *Zap!* Before you could say "self-empowerment," Jach was channeling an entity named Lazaris and signing six-figure contracts for books and tapes.

And the same thing can happen to you *if you're open to it*. All you need is a few celebrity believers (or just Shirley MacLaine), an entity, an accent, and enough platitudes about global harmony to fill a room.

So if you're stuck in a dead-end job (but have nothing against working with dead people), get into channeling now—and join the ranks of those already smiling benevolently all the way to enlightenment on paths paved with gold.

▲

35

RAMTHA: THE MAN, THE MANICURIST

A CLASSIC EXAMPLE of New Age intermediary success is that of former manicurist J.Z. Knight. No one really knows why a 35,000-year-old man decided one day to enter this thirtysomething-year-old woman—and, oddly enough, no one seems to care. Ramtha, the man, and J.Z., the ex-manicurist, are the hottest coupling to hit the channeling circuit in eons!

They met several years ago in J.Z.'s kitchen. Ironically, she was fooling around with her husband at the time. Exactly what they were doing is unclear, but a paper pyramid, which for some reason she had donned as a hat, suddenly fell over her face and caused the couple to laugh hysterically. When she lifted the pyramid and wiped her eyes, she saw a very large, glittering male entity standing next to her refrigerator. He smiled and said: "I am Ramtha, the Enlightened One. I have come to help you over the ditch."

With a line like that—even though the guy was 35,000 years old and wanted her body—how could she refuse? Encouraged by her husband, J.Z. quickly became a proficient cataleptic (trancing out to give her unexpected spirit guide his space) as well as a very, very wealthy businesswoman.

As for Ramtha, the man once known in fabled Lemuria as "the Ram," he now strides happily before large audiences in J.Z.'s clothes.

36

SPIRIT GUIDES AND GUIDELINES

WHATEVER KIND of spirit guide you're seeking to help you "over the ditch" and avoid life-flunking, there are several good paths to follow—and one rather poor one. *Don't* use the Yellow Pages.

If a spirit guide suddenly appears in your kitchen or while you're napping, fine. If not, you can choose from an abundance of enlightened deceased residing on the astral plane. Be aware, though, that finding the right entity for *you* can be tricky. (Not every 2,000-year-old man is a Ramtha or a Seth, as attested to by Mel Brooks.) You have to remember, just because someone's dead doesn't mean he or she's got the answers.

Recommendations from shamans, monks, gurus, Native-American healers, swamis, yogis, your higher self or any accredited visionary are okay—but you should still check them out.

What to Look for in an Entity*

- Affiliation with a reputable channel
- At least 1,000 years—or 200 lifetimes—of experience
- Residency certification from an accredited planetary power point (i.e., Peru, Tibet, Egypt, Atlantis)
- An accent you can understand
- Reasonable rates

*A non-being being; someone who isn't but is; someone who *was* yet *is.*

37

REACH OUT
AND TOUCH
SOMEONE DEAD

IF YOU'VE HAD NO LUCK finding a spirit guide but feel that you'd have a better shot at avoiding reincarnation if you could reach out and touch *someone* dead, you might consider holding a séance. This form of paranormal ghostnost has been a popular do-it-yourself intermediary-type pursuit for years.

Séances are like Halloween parties without costumes, and you never know who will drop in. This, of course, is their whole purpose and half the fun. (To this day, no one knows what the other half is.)

A successful séance requires: one medium, psychic, channel, clairvoyant, clairaudient, telepath, shaman or witch doctor; a round table; a dark room; 12 guileless guests; plenty of booze (receptivity to spirits increases with increased intakes of spirits); and sufficient manifestations of rapping or table-tapping to impress everyone on hand.

A successful séance does not require a caterer or a natural sense of rhythm.

38

TELEPATHY OR CALL WAITING

IT OBVIOUSLY HELPS TO be psychically well endowed if you want to avoid life-flunking, but being telepathic is like having a cellular phone in your head. The advantages of this for stockbrokers, doctors and tow-truck operators are undeniable, but since no significant incidences of ESP have ever been reported in these groups, the point is moot and the problems remain for the rest of us.

Essentially, telepathy is a brain beeper that operates day and night and can annoy telepather and telepathee alike. Sure it's free, but then so is side-stream smoke—and who needs it? Unlike call waiting, telepathy can't be discontinued or ignored. If someone wants to contact you, *you're contacted.* You could be in the middle of sex, a movie, on a desert island—you could even be dead and they'll reach you! One can only hope that with all the new high-tech psychic research, it won't be long before they come up with an extrasensory answering machine.

39

DEATH AS A WAY OF LIFE

SHAMANISM HAS BEEN dedicated for centuries to helping people get ready to die. Because death is a part of life (albeit the downside), getting it right is just as important for avoiding reincarnation, which is why shamanism, like channeling, has become such a profitable New Age profession.

It's actually as easy to become a shaman as to consult one *if* you don't mind getting into altered states of consciousness (by listening to throbbing drums or taking psychedelics), tripping into another reality to make contact with spirit entity "power" animals (not made by Mattel) and serving others before yourself (which is not only polite but advisable, considering the no-return policies of the business).

Unfortunately, because shamanism is always practiced in an altered state, it's recommended *only as a part-time job*. Making it a full-time career could be spiritually, emotionally and financially devastating—to say nothing of leaving you loony-tunes from here to eternity!

40

DRESSING FOR SPIRITUAL SUCCESS

THERE IS ONLY ONE RULE: Never wear anything you wouldn't want to be caught dead in.

41

HOW TO TELL IF YOU'VE LIVED BEFORE

EVER SINCE SHIRLEY MACLAINE told the world that she'd discovered she was once raised by a bull elephant, raped as a nomad from Mongolia, and abducted by an eagle and deposited with a primitive African family, the pursuit of past lives has become one of the New Age's most popular and pricey pastimes. The truth is, there's no *need* to spend half your life—and disposable income— trying to find out whether you've lived before. If you have, you have. Water under the cosmic bridge.

Nonetheless, for you die-hards who *simply must know before you go again* (and any mildly curious skeptics), the following Personal Reincarnation Quiz (PRQ) has been designed to simplify the process.

Answering "yes" to any of the following PRQ questions means you probably have lived before. Answering "yes" to all of them means you can be sure of it!

Your Personal Reincarnation Quiz

- When perusing a map, do you find yourself looking for the shortest route to India?
- Whenever you see a fire, do you feel like playing a fiddle?

- Do you secretly believe that the earth is flat?
- Do you experience nostalgia when seeing Mayan, Aztec, Greek or Roman ruins?
- Have you ever had the urge to fly a kite in a thunderstorm?
- Are you afraid to walk into a garage on St. Valentine's Day?
- Do you frequently remind yourself of someone else?
- Do you frequently remind someone else of someone else?
- Do you frequently forget who you are?
- Instead of watering your lawn, do you do a rain dance?
- Do you remember the Alamo—vividly?
- Do you remember Venus de Milo with arms?
- Are there rust spots on your aura?

▲

42

GETTING AHEAD WITH PAST-LIFE REGRESSION

THOUGH VASTLY overrated, finding out who you used to be—whether through rebirthing, hypnosis, dreamwork, bodywork, acupuncture or your grandmother—has its advantages insofar as becoming a better person and getting life right this time around is concerned.

If, for instance, you discovered that you were once a leper, you'd probably never again get upset over a little zit.

If you knew you were once the pampered favorite of Louis XIV, you'd probably have much nicer things to say about the French.

If you knew you were once a member of the Donner party, you'd be a little more tolerant of nonvegetarians.

If you knew you were once Vincent van Gogh, you wouldn't ever turn a deaf ear to struggling artists.

If you knew you were once Cleopatra, you'd feel worthy of being treated royally.

If you knew you were once Napoleon, you'd have a greater appreciation of the little things in life.

If you knew you were once a galley slave, you

wouldn't waste self-improvement time on a rowing machine.

If you knew you were once Houdini, you'd trust yourself to get out of tricky situations.

If you knew you were once Joan of Arc, you'd want nothing more than to stop smoking.

If you knew you were once Hannibal, you'd never make mountains out of molehills.

If you knew you were once Anne Boleyn, *all you would think of is getting a head!*

43

NEW, IMPROVED SPIRITUAL CLEANSERS

CLEANSING THE SPIRIT through meditation, yoga or any New Age discipline is a basic metaphysical hygiene. A recognized essential for personal transformation and unfoldment, it rids you of karma-clogging negative energy, which is responsible for most unwanted incarnations.

Because the life-improving potential of spiritual cleansing is unlimited, its commercial potential has not gone unnoticed. Consumers can soon expect a wide variety of prepackaged spiritual cleansers to hit the market. Among those already in the works are:

- Avatar-in-a-drum
- No-buff Karma wax
- Clip-on T'ai Chi
- Concentrated meditation
- Lemon-fresh mandalas
- All-natural rebreath mints
- Transpersonal douches
- Soft-scrub Shiatsu massage creams
- All-purpose Akido
- Pure and natural chakra moisturizers
- Acupressure gauges
- Unscented bodywork
- 99 and 44/100% pure bliss

44

CRYSTALS CLARIFIED

GETTING LIFE RIGHT can become crystal clear if you use the right crystals. And that's a big if, because confusion about crystals abounds. The reason for this is that all crystals are not the same. The difference between rose quartz and garnet, for instance, can be as great as that between Billy and Baccarat, although you can never go wrong with Baccarat (especially for protection from want). The thing to remember is that crystals, gems, stones, rocks, whatever you want to call them, all have *their own special vibratory characteristic* ("vibe") that acts as a magnet and amplifier for different kinds of energy. This can bring owners everything from enlightenment and a Mercedes to desperation and a tax audit, depending on compatibility and usage.

Person-gem compatibility (if it works for you, you're compatible; if it doesn't, you're not) is essential for reaping positive rewards. But stones have different effects on different people, and can also be used for negative purposes (as evidenced by thousands of mysteriously broken windshields each year), so know what you're doing before you cast your first one.

What You Should Know

- Never let other people touch your rocks! These stones vibrate to *your* personal energy, the way bristles on

▲

your toothbrush vibrate when you brush your teeth, and you don't want it mixed with someone else's psychic saliva.

- To be effective, any crystal or gem must be carried within three feet of the person it belongs to. For this reason, you should wear or carry yours—or a yard-stick—at all times.

- Clear white quartz crystal is the most versatile stone for all needs. It not only heightens psychic awareness and increases spirituality, but can also aid in telepathy, healing and prosperity, as well as in the finding of soul-mates, contact lenses, car keys, remote controls, tops of pens, exact change and very important phone numbers.

- Crystals and gems vary in concentrations of power as well as price, so don't expect an epiphany from a two-dollar rock.

- Growing your own crystals from premixed chemicals, which takes about a week, is a waste of seven days and not recommended for anyone under or over the age of 12 with a functioning brain or a working TV.

Crystal Caveat: *The protective powers of a crystal may be greatly reduced if hung from a car's rear-view mirror, where it can refract rays and look like a policeman's flashing blue light—causing very negative emissions (frequently in the form of curses) from the vehicle in front.*

45

PYRAMID PRESSURE

PYRAMIDS, LIKE CRYSTALS, are energy enhancers. Allegedly shaped to trap, resonate and amplify specific modes of vibrations—as well as sharpen razors and keep dairy products from spoilage—their potential in maximizing your potential for getting life right is unquestioned (although unsubstantiated) in the New Age.

Unfortunately, when the Egyptians built the Great Pyramid at Giza as an above-ground interment place for Pharaoh Cheops, they didn't know what an addictively marketable design they'd come up with. Otherwise, they wouldn't have had to ride around on camels for 73,000 years.

Pyramid-shaped objects are now being used and abused by confused, hooked millions for everything from heightening psychic awareness and filtering coffee to playing Trivial Pursuit and keeping traffic in one lane during road construction.

Fortunately, despite widespread acceptance of the purported power of pyramids, there has been no significant rise in A-line dresses or beehive hairdos.

46

UTTERLY DIVINE DIVINATIONS

MOST EVERYONE HAS a desire to know what tomorrow will bring, as evidenced by the rising salaries of TV weatherpersons. But alongside meteorology and the major arts of divination—astrology, cartomancy, palmistry—there are numerous minor divinatory arts scattered through the ages that have been used to obtain knowledge of the unknown by means of omens that have proven to be just as accurate and equally effective in preventing reincarnation. So if one form of divination doesn't work for you, don't be disheartened. There's always another.

Pyromancy, or divination by fire, was popular in ancient Rome, in London in 1666, in Chicago in 1871, and is still used in parts of the South Bronx today. Hydromancy, divination by rainwater, was the thing for about 40 days in biblical times and in Johnstown in 1889. Geomancy, divination by handfuls of earth, has been practiced by kids for centuries, and aeromancy, divination by air phenomena is said to be favored by modern-day pilots and politicians.

With the advent of the New Age, however, there has been a slew of utterly divine new ways to determine your destiny. Among them are:

- Sushimancy: divination by raw fish
- Pastamancy: divination by Italian noodles

- Cappuccinomancy: divination by steamed coffee grounds
- Armanimancy: divination by expensive men's clothing
- Ed McMahoncy: divination by Publishers' Clearing House sweepstake entries
- Clemancy: divination by liberals
- Evianamancy: divination by natural spring water
- Filofaxamancy: divination by trendy appointment books
- LeCirquemancy: divination by four-star restaurants
- Macromancy: divination by health food (or plant holders)
- Dasher, Dancer and Prancermancy: divination by reindeer
- Chancymancy: divination by dice
- Nancymancy: divination by red designer dresses
- Fancyshmancy: divination by costume jewelry
- Answermancy: divination by questions

▲

47

ASTRO-BUCK ASTROLOGY

THE POSITION OF the planets at the moment of your birth affects everything in your life. Any astrologer will tell you that heredity and environment are mere banjos compared to the humongous stringed instrument, known as our solar system, that emits vibrations down from the cosmos into each age, culture and individual—influencing our biorhythms, sex preferences, salaries, digestion, ability to eat with chopsticks, sculpt with chain saws, and more, much more.

The reason astrologers know this is because it's their business to know it. (They are *astrologers,* after all!) And with the growing concern about getting through life without flunking, as well as mounting popular desire to meet Shirley MacLaine on the astral plane, business has never been better. Aside from appearing in thousands of newspapers and magazines, horoscopes are now being printed on everything from calendars and coffee cups to tea cozies and toilet paper. We're talking astro-buck astrology!

The sky's the limit when it comes to prophecies and profits. For a fee, astrologers will tell you whatever you want to know (who you are; what your love life is like; what foods, supplements, colors, plants, pets and partners are compatible with your sun, moon and rising sign; whether it's the wrong day to look for bargains or the right day to bomb Libya). The only problem is that these stargazing soothsayers say it in "astrologese," and you haven't a *clue* if you're getting good news or bad.

The following basic, unisign interpretations are not guaranteed for future hereafters, but they should enable you at least to get your money's worth in the here and now.

It's good news if:

Jupiter is on your Venus and trining your moon.
(The stars are in your court. Go for that love match. Double your pleasure. You can bet your bottom dollar that you won't get caught.)

Pluto trines your sun.
(Power is yours. You can get whatever you want—and not have to pay until after Christmas.)

Neptune is in Capricorn.
(Dreams become reality. Your pillow talk takes on new meaning; it's time to pop for an 800 phone number.)

Mars, Pluto and the Sun form a grand trine.
(Empowerment! The tops in potential! It doesn't get better than this—unfortunately.)

It's bad news if:

Saturn sits on your Venus.
(Your love life is history.)

Mercury is in retrograde.
(If you think things are going well—you're wrong.)

Mercury opposes Pluto.
(Trouble coming. Duck now.)

Mars squares Uranus.
(Discord. Tragedy. Bad time for reconciliations and high colonics.)

▲

48

THE ZODIAC: NEW CELESTIAL REASONINGS

THERE ARE 12 SIGNS of the zodiac, giving astrologers a dozen different ways to divine for astro-bucks and everyone a 12-to-1 shot at sharing Shirley MacLaine's daily (Taurus) destiny. Knowing your sign—along with its major attributes—is as important in this lifetime as knowing your name and zip code. It's your cosmic dog tag, your celestial ID. It's how you're sized up at parties by total strangers and the only way to tell which horoscope you're supposed to read.

In keeping with New Age alternative practices (see Chapter 66), the following zodiac profiles have been arranged in alphabetical (as opposed to solar-sequential) order and focused on predictions of your reincarnation potential (RIP).

AQUARIUS. **January 21–February 19.** You are friendly, communicative, independent, intuitive, broad-minded, tactless and flighty. *RIP:* After your death, you will take up residence on the astral plane and become a very interesting but annoying channeled entity.

ARIES. **March 21–April 20.** You are innovative, alert, artistic, temperamental, self-confident and self-centered. You believe you're a superior being and feel that

▲

the earth is beneath you. *RIP:* If you don't start rearranging your priorities, your chances of avoiding reincarnation are a snowball's in hell.

CANCER. June 22–July 23. You are sympathetic, nostalgic, feeling, nurturing, accumulating, insecure, food-oriented and self-indulgent. You think that by skipping a meal you're alleviating world hunger. *RIP:* Start expanding your consciousness, not your waistline, if you want to fit through those pearly astral gates.

CAPRICORN. December 22–January 20. You are determined, organized, ambitious, hard-working, structured, dependable, self-sacrificing, time-oriented, competitive and rigid. *RIP:* Lighten up, or you'll be out of here before rigor mortis sets in and back before you know it.

GEMINI. May 21–June 21. You are quick-witted, changeable, versatile, inquisitive, talkative, easily distracted and superficial. Half the time your left brain doesn't know what your right brain is doing. *RIP:* Get that upstairs gray matter in sync fast or your afterlife won't be worth two bits.

LEO. July 24–August 23. You are playful, entertaining, loving, impressive, attention-getting, willful and egotistical. You think of acupuncture meridians as punch lines and reincarnations as encores. *RIP:* The laugh's on you; you'll be back.

LIBRA. September 24–October 23. You are balanced, impartial, cooperative, socially aware, peaceful, companionable, indecisive and wussy. You would—and would like to—save the world but don't know where to start. *RIP:* No ifs about it. At first you won't succeed, so be prepared to try and try again.

PISCES. February 20–March 20. You are sensitive, meditative, compassionate, aesthetic, dreamy, secluded, superconscious, self-effacing and guilty. You care enough to do the very best, but your hallmark is gloomy. Your inner blubbering is understandable but grating. *RIP*: If you don't stop fishing for pity and start saving the whales while you can, your chances of avoiding reincarnation are about as good as Captain Ahab's.

SAGITTARIUS. **November 23–December 21.** You are exuberant, jovial, expansive, optimistic, generous, inventive, energetic, ethical, judgmental, hypocritical and an exaggerator. You're so full of yourself—and it—you'd need booster rockets to have an out-of-body experience. *RIP*: Until you learn to buckle up your ego, forget about a seat on the astral plane.

SCORPIO. **October 24–November 22.** You are intense, passionate, mysterious, sexual, forceful, compulsive and sarcastic. You have a perverse interest in strip mining. You never conserve energy and think of reincarnation as a perpetual orgasm. *RIP*: You were born to come again and again.

TAURUS. **April 21–May 20.** You are persistent, thorough, reliable, affectionate, practical, unyielding, opinionated, possessive and materialistic. You can afford to have things your way and frequently ask for your sushi well done. *RIP*: You're a karma-kazi reincarnationalist if there ever was one.

VIRGO. **August 24–September 23.** You are methodical, intelligent, logical, analytical, neat, friendly, courteous, shy, nitpicking and fussy. You return messages from your higher self immediately and pray that there are Filofaxes after death. *RIP*: Certain.

49

Palm Reading or Hand Job— You Be the Judge

Palm readers, sometimes called chiromancers or chirognominists (though never to their faces), are essentially hands-on astrologers who call fingers by the names of planets, pass judgment on the proportions of joints and readily dole out advice on your past, your future and your chances of avoiding reincarnation if you're willing to slip them some skin and open your wallet.

There's nothing wrong with this if:

- You can afford it.
- You feel someone else knows the back of your hand better than you do.
- You go along with the belief that the hand is actually a miniature map of your inner self, that its shape and markings hold the key to your destiny, and that an extended Saturn (middle finger) reflects qualities of career and ambition.
- You're not ticklish.

50

COUNTING ON NUMEROLOGY

DON'T!

This disturbing divinatory art turns life into lotto. Based on the vibratory power of numbers, it reduces all those above 9 to a single digit. For example, the number 10 (1 + 0) becomes 1; 11 (1 + 1) becomes 2; 12 (1 + 2) becomes 3, and so on. In other words, if you were born on September 4, 1956, your life cycle number is 7 (the number of the month, date and year totaled and reduced to one digit). But in order to divine your chances of avoiding reincarnation, you have to check out the meaning of your number with a numerologist or in one of numerous numerology guides (containing varying interpretations) and then figure out the meaning of the meaning, which is just as confusing as it sounds and *could take you a lifetime!*

Although numerology very well might, as alleged, symbolize the unity and wholeness of life, and even help the mathematically inclined to avoid life-flunking, it has more drawbacks than a repossession agency:

If you go along with numerology, a $120,000 a year income would come out to be three bucks.

No one would ever be old enough to drive.

One out of every nine people in the world would have the same birthday.

On the upside, though, there is this: *a journey of a thousand miles would be a lot shorter.*

51

How to Rune a Relationship

IF YOU FEEL ASTROLOGY is too spacey and numerology too confusing to help you make the right life choices, there are always runes. Runes are ancient Teutonic characters carved in stones. Being ancient, these characters are crudely symbolic of animals or objects and have been used—primarily by women (truth!)—as a means of divination for centuries.

This century is no exception.

Unfortunately, interpretation of these crude symbols is in the eye of the beholder. An ox, for instance, can be interpreted as stupidity or virility, a door as being an obstacle to pleasure or a gateway to ecstasy, and so on. Therefore, casting runes to find out if a guy's going to be good in bed or limp pasta is okay if you just want to get your rocks off—but not for holding a potentially great relationship together.

52

THE PEOPLE'S NUMBER BOOK OF REVELATION

THE LAST BOOK of the New Testament, Revelation, has been the subject of cabalistic debates, on reincarnationalists' reading lists, and fodder for numerologists in search of getting life right since it was written. Filled with visions, dramatic portrayals of good triumphing over evil, veiled symbolism and the distinct recurrence of the number *seven,* it is a mysterious prophetic work. The *People's Number Book of Revelation* is not.

The following excerpts are from the latter.

Did you know that . . .
Elizabeth Taylor, who was born on the twenty-*seventh* day of February, was married *seven* times?

Did you know that . . .
Francis Ford Coppola's film *Apocalypse Now* was released in 19*7*9? And that *seven* of his best movies were made in the *seventies*?

Did you know that . . .
Sean Connery played secret agent James Bond, 00*7*, *seven* times?

Did you know that . . .
Yul Brynner, the actor of somewhat mysterious back-

▲

ground who was one of _seven_ stars in *The Magnificent Seven*, died in 198<u>7</u>?

Did you know that . . .
Walt Disney's *Snow White and the _Seven_ Dwarfs* was first released in 193<u>7</u>?

Did you know that . . .
Rudolph Valentino, the star of the original film *The Four Horsemen of the Apocalypse,* had _seven_ letters in his first name?

Do you care?

▲

53

I CHING, YOU CHING, WE ALL CHING

CONSULTING THE I CHING is one of the oldest, most widely used and frequently mispronounced forms of divination. (It's actually *Yee Jing*; rhymes with "peeking" or "Peking.") For nearly 5,000 years great thinkers, statesmen, psychologists, literary agents, accountants and untold millions have relied for advice on the I Ching's 64 hexagrams (which look like bar codes and are about as easy to decipher), and this is pretty remarkable considering they were developed from the markings on the back of a tortoise! Then again, it's probably as good a way of foretelling the future as stars, numbers, hands and stones.

There are several methods of consulting the I Ching. You have the original casting of yarrow stalks, which is like a complicated version of pick-up sticks, but this takes so long (and how many people have yarrow stalks lying around?) that by the time you figure out your answer, you've forgotten your problem. Then there's the bronze coin or three-penny method, and the six-wand or six-penny method. Simpler, yes; clearer, no.

Is the I Ching first-person singular? Is it even for you? Well, if you don't mind an oracle that gives answers like "He sacrifices the ram easily" and "The gourd is hidden beneath the leaves that are wrapped around it" to a simple question like "Should I serve red wine with fish?" then it definitely is. If, on the other hand, you're seeking more concrete advice on such matters as health, wealth and spiritual happiness, I suggest you contact a physician, a stockbroker and your higher self—in that order.

Proposed interpretation of hexagram #65:
Turtles make better soup than they do oracles.

54

STRAIGHT TAROT

IF YOU WANT TO KNOW whether or not reincarnation is in the cards for you, or how to deal yourself a better life, you don't have to be a fortuneteller. Just buy yourself a Tarot deck. Be forewarned, though, that there are more interpretations of the Tarot than there are of all the Beatles songs put together, and you could waste an eternity trying to divine the cards' "*real* meaning" for you. Fortunately, there's no need to.

Although a full Tarot deck actually consists of 78 cards, divided into two general sections (56 minor and 22 major arcana), no one these days plays with a full deck.

In fact, using only 21 of the major arcana, listed below, is sufficient for determining who you are and what's in store for you in this life. Since one picture is worth a thousand words (most of them arcane), the following interpretations have been appropriately updated and shortened.

THE JUGGLER: You can handle marriage, career and kids with ease. (*If card appears upside down:* You can't even boil water and chew gum at the same time.)

THE HIGH PRIESTESS: You know all and see all. (*If card appears upside down:* You're a yenta.)

THE EMPRESS: You are always at the helm of your palace. (*If card appears upside down:* Your coffers will be depleted by the IRS.)

THE EMPEROR: You will luxuriate in expensive new clothes. (*If card appears upside down:* No one will even notice what you wear.)

THE POPE: You will be worshiped for your wisdom from afar and drive a funny little car. (*If card appears upside down:* You will be arrested as a transvestite in Rome, and stoned.)

THE LOVERS: Marriage and happiness are in the offing. (*If card appears upside down:* It's time to contact Jacoby & Meyers.)

THE CHARIOT: A long journey is foretold. (*If card appears upside down:* Your transmission is shot.)

JUSTICE: A lost object will be returned to you by someone you tipped well. (*If card appears upside down:* Forget about seeing your wallet or credit cards again.)

THE HERMIT: A happy, sensitive, single person will enter your life. (*If card appears upside down:* You'll be mugged by a homeless bum.)

THE WHEEL OF FORTUNE: You will soon be surrounded by beautiful, expensive merchandise. (*If card appears upside down:* You'll go bankrupt and be laughed at by Vanna White.)

STRENGTH: You can do more than you think you can. (*If card appears upside down:* You're going to give yourself a hernia.)

THE HANGED MAN: Necking is your favorite pastime. (*If card appears upside down:* Don't act as your own attorney.)

▲

DEATH: An old problem will disappear from your life. (*If card appears upside down:* It's time to buy a plot for your mother-in-law.)

TEMPERANCE: You *can* just say no. (*If card appears upside down:* You not only can't get on the wagon—you can't get out of the gutter.)

THE DEVIL: You enjoy a little mischief now and then. (*If card appears upside down:* You're a hell-raiser.)

THE FIRE FROM HEAVEN: Every day of your vacation will be warm and cloudless. (*If card appears upside down:* Be prepared for sun poisoning.)

THE STARS: You will mix and mingle with Hollywood celebrities. (*If card appears upside down:* You'll be a waiter at Spago.)

THE MOON: You will cultivate a shimmering radiance. (*If card appears upside down:* You will develop a skin condition and be called "Crater Face.")

THE SUN: You are fiery and brilliant. (*If card appears upside down:* You're hot-tempered and stupid.)

THE JUDGMENT: You excel at making decisions. (*If card appears upside down:* You always make the wrong ones.)

THE WORLD: You are solid, purposeful and grounded in reality. (*If card appears upside down:* Running in circles is your way of getting around.)

The only thing you have to know about the minor arcana is this: whether you have five rods, swords, cups or coins, you're not going to beat a full house—or a stacked deck.

▲

55

PSYCHIC PHENOMENA TO DIE FROM

PSYCHIC (OR PSI) phenomena have been around as long as the wheel. These paranormal occurrences can't be logically explained, denied, or kept off the front pages of tabloids. (DEAD TEACHER MARKS PAPERS FROM GRAVE! HUSBAND DISAPPEARS BEFORE WIFE'S EYES! WOMAN GIVES BIRTH TO TWINS—ONE IS IDENTICAL!) are meal tickets for all types of extrasensory intermediaries—and have made Geraldo, Oprah, Phil and the New Age what they are today.

Among those to die from are:

- Supernatural childbirth
- Apparitions—if seen at a nuclear waste site
- Poltergeists—if TV is not unplugged
- ESP (extrasensory perception)—by sniffing glue
- Clairaudience—if you're a stand-up entity
- Telepathy—if thoughts could kill
- Levitation—without a net
- Automatic writing—if a presidential death threat
- Automatic speaking—if using someone else's tongue
- PK, or psychokinesis (the ability of the mind to move matter)—when the matter is life or death
- Materialization—if material is polyester
- Spontaneous human combustion

▲

56

THE ASTRAL PROJECTION– DOLBY SOUND CONNECTION

ASTRAL PROJECTION, or out-of-body experience, is a phenomenon that occurs when your corporeal body is asleep and your mind is awake—a state easily achieved through hypnosis, trance induction, deep meditation, hallucinogenic drugs or New Age music.

Because your astral body is an exact replica of your physical one, only invisible, you can learn all you need to know about getting life right without moving a muscle. You can fly, pass through walls, talk to departed spirits, travel anywhere (even take a peek at the astral plane) for free, and never need a change of underwear. A silver cord (like those retractable ones on vacuum cleaners, only infinitely longer) used to connect the astral and physical bodies. Shirley MacLaine still uses one for her out-of-body forays, but most astral projection today is cordless.

Dolby sound comes from a noise suppressor that cuts out invisible high frequencies and causes your records, tapes and CDs to come across so amazingly clear that you think the artists are right in the room with you. Phenomenal as this is, there is no known connection between astral projection and Dolby sound.

57

OUT-OF-BODY EXPERIENCES OF A LIFETIME

THE GREATEST OUT-OF-BODY experiences (OBEs) are those you hardly ever hear about. This is not because they aren't helpful in avoiding life-flunking but because so few people have them, and most of those who do are now heavily sedated. But the potential joys of slipping out of a corporeal body and into a second, astral body are—though notably undocumented—numerous.

Out-of Body Experiences of a Lifetime

Out-of-body orgasm (good for the two of you)
Out-of-body sunbathing (no clothes or sunscreen required)
Out-of-body dieting (a piece of cake)
Out-of-body car insurance (no collision needed)
Out-of-body building (no weights—or permits)
Out-of-body orthodontia (no unsightly braces)
Out-of-body clothes shopping (no waiting for a dressing room)
Out-of-body skiing (no waiting in lift lines)
Out-of-body surveillance (outta sight!)

58

NEAR-DEATH EXPERIENCES: GOD'S IOUs

NEAR-DEATH EXPERIENCES (NDEs) are cosmic "close calls": out-of-body experiences (OBEs) for the clinically dead but not gone, heaven-sent second chances for taking the test of life again and passing. Hundreds of NDEs are reported every year, which means a lot of people have plenty to be thankful for—although often a tendency to be a *teensy* bit smug about their sneak preview of the afterlife.

But just because you've never been sucked through a long, dark tunnel, admired your own corpse or met a warm, indescribable "being of light" doesn't mean you haven't had an NDE. Chances are, you've probably had more than you can—or care to—remember.

Some near-death experiences you might have forgotten:

- Almost being strangled by your umbilical cord
- Almost being strangled by your brother
- Almost buying a vacation home on Three-Mile Island
- Almost having sex with an IV drug user
- Almost choking on your mother's pot roast
- Almost putting a knife in the toaster
- Almost wearing the same outfit as Barbara Bush

59

ATLANTIS ON $5 A DAY

WIDELY ACCEPTED AS having once been the height of all civilization, the birthplace of crystal power and the former home of many spirit entities, Atlantis is revered by the New Age for having spawned the civilizations of Central America, Mexico and Peru, as well as inspiring much of Shirley MacLaine's past-life exploration. Quite the happening place in its heyday, it volcanically self-destructed eons ago and sank into the ocean with all its inhabitants because of their opprobrious misuse of power. If nothing else, Atlantis is a prime example of flunking at life.

Getting There

Located east of the sun and west of the Strait of Gibraltar beneath the gently undulating waves of the beautiful Atlantic Ocean, this magical, submerged lost continent is easily reached from any global power point. For the trip of a lifetime, consult your astral travel agent for departure dates and group or student discounts.

What to Take with You

Scuba-diving gear for day and evening; wet suits suitable for hiking, mystic rituals and high-spirited parties; $5.

What to See

The Sanctuary of Cleito and Poseidon. Poseidon's own

temple, one of Atlantis' main attractions; conveniently located in the center of the City of the Golden Gates. The sanctuary's exterior is entirely covered with silver, its pinnacles with gold, and to build it today would cost more than the national debt. The interior, all ivory, gold and silver, contains a statue of Poseidon that should not be missed—*and can't be!* It's a colossal rendering of the sea god in a chariot drawn by winged horses, surrounded by a hundred nymphets riding dolphins, and it makes Michelangelo's *David* look like a hood ornament. Gift shop sells dolphin paraphernalia, trident scepters, crystals, "I- ♥ Divine Wisdom" T-shirts, and advertises life-size plastic replicas of the Poseidon statue as a joke. Open daily. Closed during fishing season and ritual sacrifices.

The Mystery Temple. Once the exclusive domain of oracles, psychics and goddesses, the Mystery Temple has become Atlantis' most popular attraction, renowned for its Crystal Chamber, a sacred consciousness-raising environment, and for its snack shop's thick Volcanic shakes. The temple is well worth the usual 20–40 minute wait in line.

The Volcano. Referred to by locals as "Big Belcher." Depending on the tide, the climb to the top takes about two hours. Inactive since 9,600 B.C., it's not all that exciting for youngsters, but a trip to Atlantis would not be complete without seeing it.

Shopping

Atlantis is famed for its unique white, black and red stone buildings, bridges and shops. Better set aside a day for leisurely browsing. Best buys are perfumes (distilled naturally from fragrant flowers by vestal virgins), precious metals, and crystals. There is no sales tax in Atlantis. Because customs officers tend to look away if you tell them you've just returned from the lost continent, you can come home with some *phenomenal* bargains!

Dining Tips

Order fish.

Getting Around

All animals on Atlantis are domesticated, and most of the big ones accept passengers—although it's sometimes difficult to find a dolphin during rush hour. Winged horses are available only if booked in advance.

Special Events

The Festival of the 10 Kings (Aug. 10–20); the Miss Atlantis Goddess pageant (Sept. 4); underwater skiing exhibitions (Sundays, 1–5 P.M.); Poseidon's Birthday (March 3); seahorse racing (June–Sept.); octopus wrestling and ritual sacrifices (daily).

▲

60

YOURS AURA
MINE

AURAS ARE LUMINOUS, radiant clouds of light (pulsing energy, actually) that surround the human body, chiefly the head. They come in a variety of colors—from "Miami Vice" pastels to Modigliani earth tones—but only clairvoyants and people who really, really, *really* want to can see them.

Since most people don't give a flying synapse whether they do or don't, they can't.

This is unfortunate because you can tell a lot about a person from his or her aura, and sizing someone up at a glance is extremely helpful in getting life right the first time. For instance, red indicates passion; yellow, intelligence; purple, high spiritual and psychic awareness. So if you're looking for a hot, smart, enlightened partner, you've got it made. Then again, since auras extend out from the body about six feet, this can cause serious color-mix conceptions in crowd situations.

On the other hand, you too are your aura, and it is a reflection of you. But my feeling is this: forget about trying to heighten your consciousness to improve your colors. Consult your hairdresser instead. If you want an aura you can be sure of, *get highlights!*

61

BARBECUED SOLES

WALKING ACROSS hot coals with bare feet used to be something done only by yogis, who used meditation to make themselves insensible to heat and pain. Today, anyone who can come up with a hundred bucks can do it.

Firewalking is supposed to convince you that you have limitless amounts of hidden courage that will enable you to turn your life around and get it right; that after having walked barefoot over hot coals, you can face death, tell off your boss, defy gravity, bend spoons, stop watches, write that book, tote that barge, lift that bale—*do anything!*

There's only one drawback: you can't dance for joy until several months afterward.

▲

62

PIE IN THE SKY
OR UFO

CLOSE ENCOUNTERS of any kind are New Age; close encounters of the third kind are *very* New Age. Between Stephen Spielberg and Shirley MacLaine (and a best-seller by Whitley Strieber), extraterrestrials have come out of the realm of science fiction and into their own as enlightened entities—intelligent and curious life-forms from other, more advanced worlds with the real lowdown on getting life right.

For years now, there have been thousands and thousands of reported sightings of unidentified objects flying through the air. Having eluded official and scientific explanation, these UFOs are generally thought to be spaceships manned by extraterrestrials.

Unfortunately, many people who have seen circular disks zipping noiselessly through the sky waste an inordinate amount of their lives wondering whether or not they've *actually seen* a flying saucer.

If you are one of these people, stop wasting your life *now*!

The rule is this: If the unidentified airborne object has flashing lights, windows, beings inside who look like Casper the ghost or mutated lizards, it's a flying saucer. If there's a dog chasing it, it's a frisbee.

63

Out of Synchronicity

Have you ever thought of an old friend whom you haven't seen in years and then just two hours (days, weeks, months) later run into that very person at a store you swore you'd never set foot in again? Sheer coincidence? No. It's "meaningful coincidence." *That's synchronicity.*

Though a fairly unremarkable phenomenon as phenomena go, Dr. Carl Jung (a zealous Capricorn) dedicated years to its study, as do numerous New Agers in workshops across the nation today.

Synchronicity is based on the assumption that there is a collective unconscious that deliberately links us to physical events. Why? That's for your unconscious to know and you to find out. (Besides, if identical thoughts occur simultaneously in two complete strangers, what business is it of yours? Unless you're one of the strangers.)

To get the most out of synchronicity, just think of all happy coincidences as invisible cosmic flowers that have drifted into your life because you're on the right path, and don't forget to smell the roses. To avoid life-flunking, of course, you have to always be in the right place at the right time.

64

SEDUCING THE UNCONSCIOUS

THE BEST WAY to seduce the unconcious is simply to slip into something more comfortable—like an altered state.

65

COSMIC JOKES

EVERYONE TALKS ABOUT "cosmic jokes," but no one ever tells them. This might be because they've never been written down. Then again, it might not. The cosmos is funny that way. In either case, here are a few for your present and afterlife edification and entertainment:

What did one spirit entity say to another?
"Take my life—please!"

Why did the medium cross the road?
To get to the other side!

What do you call a fortuneteller who's just had a baby?
A crystal-packin' momma.

How do spiritualists travel?
On transpersonal airlines.

Why is gambling barred in Atlantean casinos?
They're under the 12-mile limit.

What makes G.E. a metaphysical corporation?
They bring good things to life.

What do you give to a sick guru?
Transcendental medication.

Did you hear about what happened to the Wall Street psychic?
He was arrested for insight trading.

What did the manager give the past-life regressionist?
A womb with a view.

▲

66

ALTERNATIVE STATES OF THE HEALING ARTS

ALL NEW AGE philosophies are rooted in oneness and dedicated to alternatives. This might sound paradoxical, but so does plastic glass—and no one questions that. The New Age wouldn't be *new* if it *wasn't* committed to alternatives! Being open to considering any and all alternatives—alternative medicine, alternative therapy, alternative religion, alternative-side-of-the-street parking—is necessary for body-mind-spirit harmony and is no less essential to a successful afterlife than dying.

Listed below are some state-of-the-arts alternatives to consider. (Consult an enlicensed metaphysician before making a commitment to any of them.)

- Transcendentisty
- Karma cardiology
- Holistic gynecology (for the total woman)
- Hermetic electrolysis
- Mandala mammography
- Synergetic rhinoplasty
- Akashic amniocentesis
- Polarity pap smears
- Kirlian Kung-Fu
- Chiroproctology
- Dharmatology
- Prenatal rebirthing
- Tibetan tine tests
- Vedic vasectomies
- Shiatsu sigmoidoscopy
- Yogaerobics
- Hakomi health insurance

67

HEALING WITH MONEY

EVER SINCE HEALING with crocodile dung and tooth of swine fell out of favor, money has been used in curing the body and mind of "dis-ease" and helping people to get life right (or at least distract them enough to not care). The time-tested healing processes of this great tradition are irrefutable, amazing, and more important today than ever before. Even the staid American Medical Association concedes that the dynamics of money and its relationship to all facets of medicine can no longer be ignored.

Shown to be effective in the treatment of all ailments, including marital and credit problems, money has also been found to help retard the aging process, promote deep feelings of well-being around tax time, and improve the general quality of life, clothing, domiciles and karma.

Because it incorporates both a physical and psychological function into an organic whole (sometimes referred to as the "bottomless whole"), healing with money is the natural therapy of choice among enlightened health—and young urban—professionals.

68

HOMEOPATHY: THE PHOBIA

NOW THAT NEW AGE alternative healing is "in," homeopaths are coming out of the closet in increasing numbers. Because of this, homeopathy phobia is, not surprisingly, on the rise among the conservative establishment. Even before Samuel Hahnemann introduced his "law of similars" in 1819, advocation of anything "capable of producing *a similar affection*" was frowned on by mainstream society.

Although many have claimed that homeopathy, which is rooted in the old "hair of the dog" philosophy, is the only enlightened and natural way to treat illness, that curing "like with like" (as in giving a tiny tincture of poison ivy to cure poison ivy) really works, one can understand its capacity to provoke morbid aversion. Let's face it, you might be able to cure a hangover with a Bloody Mary—but prescribing an ocean cruise as an antidote for seasickness is pushing it!

69

Flower-Healing Arrangements

SENDING FLOWERS to sick people to speed their recovery has been a common practice for years, but it has nothing to do with New Age flower healing. This floral alternative to mainstream medicine involves putting drops of tinctures made from petals and buds under a patient's tongue to put the bloom back in that patient's cheeks.

There's little doubt that roses are a fine cure for the blues, but there's little evidence that a mouthful of them will cure anything—except, perhaps, bad breath. As far as getting life right this time around and flower healing are concerned, I think you'll find that better arrangements can be made through an FTD florist.

70

REBIRTHING CONTROL

NEGATIVE THOUGHTS, according to New Age rebirthers dedicated to healing, are created not only during childhood but also at birth, during pregnancy and even at conception. (In fact, the reason you might feel unloved, unwanted and unworthy could be that your mom said "Not tonight, honey" and your dad didn't listen.) Rebirthers contend that these destructive views of the self operate as "personal laws" and screw up your chances of getting life right by causing all sorts of phobias (fear of bright lights, white sheets, pats on the tush, etc.) but *can* be neutralized by *breathing* your way back to the original trauma.

Talk about taking the lung way home!

Heavy breathing is one thing, but my advice is this: if you have a choice of going back to the womb or back to the Bahamas, take the Bahamas. And if you're hoping to avoid reincarnation through rebirthing—well, don't hold your breath.

71

STRESS REDUCTION THROUGH DREAMWORK

NEW AGERS ARE OBSESSED with reducing stress, *all* stress, in their lifetime and yours. While this has a lot to do with getting life right, you don't need a neurolinguistic programmer, a hypnotist or a shrink to tell you there's nothing like a good night's sleep to reduce stress. And anyway, they'll tell you that dreams are WATS lines to your unconscious, messages from your higher self, pre-recorded nightly illuminators just waiting to help you overcome everything from the fear of flying to Big Mac attacks—providing you *work with them.*

Ay, there's the rub.

Before you go to sleep, you have to remember to remember your dreams. When you wake up, you have to remember to write them down. After remembering to remember them and remembering to write them down, you have to remember why you were supposed to work with them in the first place—which can cause more stress than you had to begin with.

My feeling is, so what if dreams hold the keys to the great cosmic elucidation washroom where all un-knowing is flushed away and you don't have a tip for a towel of enlightenment. I say, if you want to reduce stress, *just get a good night's sleep.*

▲

72

Relaxing Is Hard Work

If there is anything other than sex that's easier said than done, it's relaxation. No matter how many times you've been lulled into la-la land by hypnotists and neurolinguistic programmers, or what you've heard from Zen Buddhists and transcendental meditators about "just saying *OM*," trust me—*relaxation is hard work under certain circumstances.*

To spare you hours of unnecessary workshops, seminars and guilt (in this or future lifetimes), I've provided some illustrations below.

It's difficult to relax when:

- Your hair is on fire.
- You're under arrest.
- Your privates are being probed with cold steel.
- Your pilot asks you to assume the crash position.
- Someone has a gun up your nose.
- Your car does a 360° wheelie.
- Your blind date comes to the door in a straitjacket.
- You show no reflection in a mirror.

73

THE ONE-MINUTE MEDITATOR

THERE'S NO LONGER any doubt that meditation reduces stress and lowers blood pressure. But aside from Tibetan monks and San Quentin lifers, *who has time for it?*

One-minute meditation, on the other hand, is a microwave for your mind. It's simple, practical, ideal for career persons on the go who want higher consciousness without stopping to achieve it. And, best of all, *it only takes a minute of your time!*

How to Do It

Step 1: Turn off the TV.

Step 2: Select a focus word that you can pronounce correctly and has a meaning for you (i.e., "Me," "Money," "More," "Now").

Step 3: Close your eyes.

Step 4: Concentrate on your breath as you slowly inhale and exhale. (You might want to keep some Tic-Tacs with you.)

Step 5: Repeat your focus word on the exhale—60 times.

There are three important things to remember about one-minute meditating, but they're as simple as ABC:

Allow yourself 60 seconds.
Begin when you're ready.
Conclude when you're done.

▲

74

HOW TO ROLF
YOURSELF

ROLFING IS THE IDEAL manipulative bodywork therapy
for masochists seeking to succeed at life without reincarnating. It's based on the premise that your physical
structure (the way you stand, the way you sit; the way
you wear your hat, the way you sip your tea) determines
how you behave and that there's no gain without pain.

By submitting yourself to excruciating pain to ex-
orcise chronic pain that allegedly lives in your body and
mind—and causes everything from insomnia and gin-
givitis to impotence and writer's block—you can rein-
tegrate, balance and optimize your mental and physical
energies. Providing, that is, you can still walk.

Rolfing yourself is a lot easier than you might think.
In fact, many home-Rolfers have achieved excellent
and speedy results by shouting racial slurs at boxing
matches, massaging their abdomens with jackhammers,
roto-tilling their thighs, blowtorching their buttocks,
and plunging hot pokers into their navels.

Your level of success, naturally, depends on your
threshold of pain.

75

KNEE-JERK REFLEXOLOGY

THIS IS SOUL-SEARCHING healing for foot fetishists.

Reflexologists hold that all nerve endings wind up in your feet, that they correspond with all your organs, and that a good foot massage can unblock energies needed to get life right, relieve pain and also produce a variety of involuntary physical responses—even orgasm. (Now you know where the G-spot is!)

For reincarnation avoidance, reflexology has its merits. As far as orgasms go, you'll probably want to stick to the old-fashioned way (and it's not by playing footsie). But if you're looking for the ultimate in safe sex in this lifetime, reflexology is something worth kicking up your heels for.

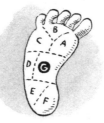

76

THE PROS AND CONS OF POLARITY THERAPY

MUCH LIKE REFLEXOLOGY, polarity therapy is based on the principle that any blockage in the body's flow of positive and negative energy can create conflict, pain and spiritual brownouts. To counteract these problems, polarity therapy requires fancy massaging footwork by the right (and left) hands.

Deciding whether or not polarity therapy is right for you is really an either-or decision.

77

BIOFEEDBACK AND FRONTAL NUDITY

BIOFEEDBACK IS ONE of the New Age's most high-tech stress-reducing tools, and there are three things you should know about it:

1. It is not a cure for bulimia.
2. It has nothing to do with organic recycling.
3. It is not what you get after burping a baby.

Basically, biofeedback is a method of monitoring your brain waves so you can tell whether you're relaxed and in a higher state of consciousness conducive to lowering your cholesterol levels (*alpha*), just awake and functioning (*beta*), in a deep meditative mode conducive to OBEs (*theta*), or zonked and out of it (*delta*). But if you can't determine this by yourself, you need more than an EEG to turn on your brights.

As far as frontal nudity goes, there are only two things you should know:

1. It's much more enlightening than frontal lobotomy.
2. It's a lot more fun than biofeedback.

78

HIP HYPNOSIS

HYPNOSIS, THE BLACK & DECKER of the New Age healing tools, is used to break bad habits, change behavior patterns, improve your karma in general, and more. But the best thing about operating on both your conscious and subconscious levels is that you're able to achieve a sensation of duality, *to find two yous in one.* (This is no big deal for natural schizophrenics, but that's their loss.)

Called "the hidden observer," this phenomenon enables you to *spy on yourself*! For instance, you can find out what it was that you really meant to say, what you were thinking of when you did something foolish, whatever it was that you were supposed to remember but forgot, and to finally relieve the tip of your tongue of all those names that have been stuck on it.

Also, because your mind is functioning on two levels simultaneously, you could try your hand at automatic writing (although I advise thinking twice before submitting it to a publisher) or simply past-life regressing for the fun of it.

The decision is between you and yourself. But whatever you do under hypnosis—*don't just lie there!*

79

THOSE RIGHT-BRAIN/ WRONG-BODY PROBLEMS

ALTHOUGH THE BRAIN has two hemispheres, New Agers feel that people who are more right-brain than left-brain have greater potential to get through life without flunking and therefore make more desirable mates. This is probably why right-brain/wrong-body problems seem to be most prevalent among partner-seeking singles. Because the right brain is creative, intuitive, metaphorical and metaphysical, right-brain people tend to be spontaneous, sensuous, inventive, charismatic, and sought after as ideal New Age soulmates.

Unfortunately, they also tend to be either happily married or complete trolls.

To solve this sort of right-brain/wrong-body problem, force yourself not to dismiss every rational, logical, pragmatic left-brain person you meet in this lifetime as unenlightened and insipid. Aside from being specious and untrue, it's discriminatory. You have to remember that we are all parts of the same whole—and never forget that half a brain is better than none!

80

GESTALT!
GOD BLESS YOU!

IF YOU'RE CONFUSED about healing therapies—and don't want to spend hundreds of hours and thousands of dollars to find the right one for you—go Gestalt. Gestalt therapy propounds wholeness and completeness, and believes in achieving insight through trusting your higher self and "doing your own thing."

There's no primal screaming, no penis envy among men, and all you have to keep in mind is the here and now and that "you are you." This is a lot simpler than having to remind yourself of the difference between an Oedipal and military-industrial complex, or even re-membering where you left off the day before.

As satisfying as a psychological sneeze, Gestalt is a therapeutic, nonviolent New Age approach to enlight-enment—*and has even been known to work!*

81

ACTUAL ACTUALIZATION

DON'T WORRY ABOUT understanding transpersonal psychology, Dr. Abraham Maslow's approach to your ultimate development as an individual *and* as a species. Although this mind-body-spirit healing therapy is the birth force behind self-actualization, and is regarded by New Agers as a steppingstone to reincarnation-preventing enlightenment, getting the gist of it is a piece of cosmic cake. In fact, self-actualization is actually nothing more than realizing and converting all that you *actually* are, through *actual* action, into all that you can *actually* be.

In other words, get real!

▲

82

PAINS IN THE CHAKRAS

HAVE YOU EVER HAD a migraine that made the top of your head feel as if it were being torn from your body? A pulsing headache between your eyes? A throat that felt as if it were lined with sandpaper? Knife-like chest pains? Upset stomach? A dull ache in your lower back? Cystitis or jock itch? If so, you know where your seven major chakras are.

Knowing *what* they are is the tricky part.

Chakras are *spiraling wheels of centered energy,* storage batteries for your life-force energy that can help you get life right. They are also power points that connect your soul (astral body/love body/plasma body/no body) to your physical body and can only be seen by clairvoyants. Extolled by New Agers as "organs of consciousness," chakras are cosmically divined counterparts of your body's nerves and glands and organs, and are absolutely pivotal to mind-body-spirit harmony, to say nothing of keeping you pulled together.

Unenlightenment, disease and reincarnation recidivism always stem from some sort of chakra blockage— or from chips off an old chakra block.

83

BALANCING AND ALIGNING ENERGIES AND TIRES

IF YOUR CAR NEEDS extra steering to keep it moving in a straight line, you know it's time to have your tires balanced and aligned. Well, if you're having problems keeping your mental, physical and spiritual self on an even keel, it's time to do the same for your "wheels of energy."

Chakra tune-ups are not hard to come by. In fact, most New Age workshops based on thousand-year-old techniques offer them in one form or another.

T'ai Chi, Akido and Raja Yoga are usually pretty good when it comes to straightening out misaligned yin-yangs, but don't expect the job to be done overnight.

If you're in a hurry for total attunement with the universe, you're probably better off with guided meditation or mantra chanting.

If you're desperate—well, there's always Rolfing.

Remember: No matter what befalls you in life, it's always easier to find a holistic workshop than a good mechanic.

84

CENTERING PUTS YOU IN THE MIDDLE

ONE OF THE MOST important elements of self-transformation, centering entails grounding your energy, being firmly at one with yourself, the trees, the planet and the cosmos. It is an acknowledged necessity for mental, physical and spiritual balance, without which we might spend endlessly recurring lifetimes tripping over our own chakras and not even know it.

The only way to learn centering—to become centered—is through continuous practice. The easiest method is to practice with a hula hoop.

85

Bioenergetics for Couch Potatoes

IF YOU'RE NOT AVERSE to pain or humiliation, and would enjoy a little respite from New Age peace, love and nonviolence in your quest for exorcising old traumas and getting life right this time, bioenergetics might be the therapy for you.

Working with an experienced bioenergetic counselor—someone with the compassion of Torquemada—is helpful in devising torturous ways to get you to release whatever energy-blocking anger is embedded in your muscle structure, but it's not really necessary.

Any couch potato with a broken remote control or poor TV reception can easily self-induce the same sort of healthy rage. Once established, all you have to do is grab a baseball bat and start bludgeoning the cushions. Then just keep slugging until your energy channels are unblocked—or until the couch is destroyed. Whatever comes sooner, works.

86

YOGA WITH A TWIST

YOGA IS SAID TO BE a metaphor for life. Whether this means that life is a series of complicated contortions or that yoga's a bitch and then you die is unclear. Either way, it's one of the most laid-back disciplines around.

Meant to rest rather than exhaust the body, yoga asanas are *slow* stretching postures that can, accompanied by *slow* methodical breathing, *slowly* relieve tension, *slowly* heighten consciousness and *slowly* increase sexual pleasure to tantric ecstacy—providing you don't fall asleep in the meantime.

The solution that I've come up with for helping you to get life right while staying awake is *yogaerobics*! Fun, and fabulous for karma-vascular circulation, yogaerobics is the mind-body-spirit workout you've been waiting for. So turn down those Tibetan bells and crank up the rock. After a thousand years of chilling out for enlightenment, it's time to kindle that kundalini fire and *"go for the burn!"*

87

PUSHPIN ACUPUNCTURE

IF YOU DON'T MIND someone needling you and you're a good sport about letting your body be used as a pincushion, acupuncture can be spiritually enlightening, physically healing, and plain old good clean-needle fun.

By poking sharp needles into the power points of your Qi (pronounced "chee," as in "Cheezus!"), which is an invisible stream of positive and negative energy that runs along equally invisibly bodily meridians, a seasoned dart doctor can help you access helpful information about former incarnations and pinpoint nettlesome karma problems before you can say "ouch."

Although this is a fast way to bring body, mind and spirit into harmony (and one of Shirley MacLaine's favorites) I, personally, prefer a pitch pipe.

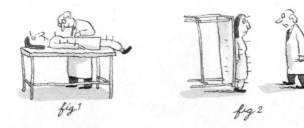

fig. 1   *fig. 2*

88

INCENSE INSENSITIVITY

BECAUSE THE NEW AGE borrows freely from Eastern religions and practices, incense burning has become its favorite mood-setting nostrum. Generally sprinkled on lighted charcoal in a censer, incense has been used in rituals throughout history as an oblation, or protection from demons, or in the hope of reviving the dead, but is now being used by New Agers for everything from achieving higher consciousness to masking unpleasant doggy odors.

One can hardly enter a health-food store, take a yoga class or buy a crystal these days without being instantly whelmed by the side-stream stench of burning resins. *Put a lid on it, guys!* Part of getting life right is being sensitive to the needs of others, and continually assaulting their nasal passages with billows of smoldering sandalwood or myrrh or thyme is not just being insensitive—*it stinks!*

89

THE TAO OF SHOPPING

THE BIG DILEMMA for budget-minded shoppers has always been having to choose between this and that. Because the very *essence* of the Tao is that the "this" is also the "that," and the "that" is also the "this," with Tao shopping *you don't have to choose*! You can buy both, because they are—metaphysically, at least—the same thing!

Tao belief holds that the only constant is change and that intuitive wisdom, rather than rational knowledge, is the way to go. So go ahead, trust yourself if you think you need a new outfit for every day of the week every week of the year. Spontaneity is actually the Tao principle of action. Called *wu-wei* in Chinese, it becomes "whoo-whee!" in Bloomingdale's pretty fast.

When the credit-card companies call and you're broke, you can always take comfort in the words of Lao Tzu, who said: "Be vacant, and you will remain full." But you should also remember the words of Mrs. L., who said: "Get whatever you want, as long as you get it wholesale."

90

WHAT'S YIN,
WHAT'S YANG,
WHAT'S OUT

THE CHINESE "Diagram of the Supreme Ultimate" (T'ai Chi Tu) looks like a black and a white tadpole getting very well acquainted. It is the universal symbol for the harmony of opposites—and the fundamental credo of the New Age.

But just because where there's a high there's a low doesn't mean two yins make a yang. So if you're seeking wholeness and balance in your life in order to get it right this time, here's an easy guide to what's yin, what's yang, and what's out.

WHAT'S YIN	WHAT'S YANG	WHAT'S OUT
Female	Male	Boy George
Negative	Positive	So-so
Passive	Active	Wussy
Earth	Heaven	Los Angeles
Dark	Light	Hazy
Soft	Hard	Orthopedic
Below and resting	Above and moving	Alone and phoning Dr. Ruth
Cold	Hot	Microwaved
Tails	Heads	Entrails

WHAT'S YIN	WHAT'S YANG	WHAT'S OUT
Fingers	Palms	Brass knuckles
Touching for health	Laying on hands	Petting
Intuitive	Logical	Nerdy
North	South	Rebel without a cause
Right brain	Left brain	Lobotomy

▲

91

DOUBLE-
DIPPED KOANS

FOR CENTURIES, Zen masters have been posing seemingly self-contradictory and absurd questions to their students to inspire them to think more deeply for centuries. Yet even after all this time—aside from "What is the sound of one hand clapping?"—most Westerners don't know a koan from a Levy.

Now, thanks to rising interest in Eastern philosophies and automotive parts, the Zen masters of motorcycle maintenance at Paul's garage and body shop in Detroit have come up with a veritable *Bhagavad-Gita* of koans tailored for New Agers hoping to pass the test of life, a dozen of which appear below.

Noted with Pressure

(For best results, these koans should be pondered with an open mind and an empty stomach.)

1. If there are 100 bottles of beer on a wall and one of these bottles happens to fall, who pays the bill?
2. If Humpty Dumpty sat on a wall, and Humpty Dumpty had a great fall, would he still have a great spring?
3. How much wood would a woodchuck chuck if a woodchuck could chuck wood?
4. If a blind bear climbed over a mountain, what *would* he see?

5. If man had no fingers, would chicken still be finger-lickin' good?
6. If the meek inherit the earth, what do the rest of us get?
7. How long do you wait if you don't go away?
8. How many pins can you sit on the head of an angel?
9. When you smell trouble, can trouble smell you?
10. If it takes one to know one, what does it take no one to do?

92

MEALTIME MANTRAS

THE CONSTANT repetition of mantras, sacred utterances containing the sacred syllable *om,* is used to focus the mind on objects of meditation and for prayers of thanksgiving. This practice, which is known in the East as *japa* but would be deemed *rapping* elsewhere, is considered by the unenlightened to be one of the most boring rituals ever witnessed. Actually it has been likened by some to listening to a scratch in a record and by others to the hum of a Hyundai engine. Nonetheless, the use of mantras for focusing on getting life right in the New Age is widespread and growing—particularly at mealtimes.

Chanting before meals not only promotes deeper spiritual awareness of the earth's bountiful riches but minimizes martini drinking, spares you from long recitations of specials at restaurants, and helps reduce blood cholesterol levels among believers.

Here are a few you can chant and chew on:

Mantra for Soups and Appetizers
"Om, om *good!* Om, om *good!*"

Mantra for Meat
"I've got a taste for om *real food."*

Mantra for Sushi
"Tekomaki, kappomaki, futomaki."

Mantra for Vegetables
"OM the valley—ho, ho, ho—om the Jolly Green Giant."

Mantra for Dairy Products
"Everything's better with Blue Bomnet om it."

Mantra for Cereals
"The breakfast om champions!"

Mantra for Fast Foods
"You . . . om . . . om . . . a break . . . om . . . today."

Mantra for Desserts
"J-E-L-L—om!"

▲

93

THE HERBAL TEA CEREMONY

THE HERBAL TEA ceremony is one of the least metaphysical and most frequently preformed New Age rituals.

It begins with the arrival of a New Age guest.

THE HOST GREETS THE GUEST BY SAYING: "I'm so glad that you and I are finally able to connect."

GUEST SAYS: "Me too."

HOST SAYS: "Would you like a cup of coffee?"

GUEST SAYS: "No, thank you."

HOST SAYS: "Decaf?"

GUEST SAYS: "No, no thank you."

HOST SAYS: "Tea?"

GUEST SAYS: "Herbal?"

HOST SAYS: "Peppermint, chamomile, cranberry cove or sleepytime."

GUEST SAYS: "Cranberry cove sounds great."

HOST SAYS: "You've got it."

AFTER THE TEA IS PREPARED, THE HOST SAYS: "Sugar?"

GUEST SAYS: "No, thank you."

HOST SAYS: "Nutra-Sweet?"

GUEST SAYS: "No."

HOST SAYS: "Honey?"

GUEST SAYS: "Just a teaspoon."

AFTER THE HONEY IS ADDED, THE HOST SAYS: "Milk?"

GUEST SAYS: "Maybe a little."

HOST POURS MILK INTO TEA AND SAYS: "Is this enough?"

GUEST LOOKS AND SAYS: "A little more."

HOST POURS MORE MILK AND SAYS: "How's this?"

GUEST SAYS: "Perfect."

HOST WAITS UNTIL GUEST TAKES A SIP OF TEA, THEN SAYS: "Is it all right?"

GUEST SAYS: "It's fine."

HOST SAYS: "I have more honey if you want."

GUEST SAYS: "No, really, this is fine."

HOST SAYS: "Are you sure? It's all natural."

GUEST SAYS: "Well . . . maybe just a drop."

HOST ADDS MORE HONEY, WAITS FOR GUEST TO TASTE TEA AGAIN, THEN SAYS: "How's that—better?"

GUEST SAYS: "Much. It's perfect. Thank you."

HOST SAYS: "Enjoy."

GUEST SAYS: "Aren't you having any?"

HOST SAYS: "Maybe later."

GUEST SAYS: "Would you like a sip of mine?"

HOST SAYS: "No, I'm fine. You drink it."

GUEST PROFFERS CUP AND SAYS: "Here. Don't be such a Taurus."

HOST TAKES A SIP AND SAYS: "Thank you for sharing that with me."

A laugh from both parties concludes the herbal tea ceremony.

94

MARTIAL VS. MARITAL ARTS

MARTIAL ARTS, such as T'ai Chi Ch'uan and Akido (geared to avoiding life-flunking through achieving inner peace and outer protection) and marital arts, such as found in the Kamasutra and *The Joy of Sex,* have many similarities.

Their similarities are:

- The importance of leverage
- Movements to lubricate every part of the body and relax the mind
- The principle of harmonizing and uniting selves
- Creative and spontaneous techniques
- Being "the ultimate unknowable source of life from which all things come"

Choosing between them depends on what position you take.

As a general rule, martial arts are performed standing up and marital arts lying down.

95

The Sayings of Confusion

Confusion (as opposed to the ancient Chinese wise man and reincarnation-avoidance New Age spokesperson with a similar name) is the embodiment of unenlightenment and has profoundly influenced moral and ethical codes of behavior for thousands of years. The Sayings of Confusion, which comprise hundreds of recorded brief interrogatives, are deceptively simple, telling, and far too numerous to be included in a single book.

For this reason, only a compressed sampling of the most familiar are presented here.

Familiar Sayings of Confusion

- Why me?
- Where am I?
- Who are you?
- Are you talking to me?
- What are we doing here?
- Why are you looking at me like that?
- What do you think you're doing?
- Who do you think you are?
- What do you think I am?
- Which way did they go?
- What's going on here?
- Why are you asking me?

- Which one is mine?
- What's that I smell?
- Was that you or me?
- What am I supposed to do about it?
- Was that who I thought it was?
- Wherever in the world did you get that idea?
- What did you mean by that?
- What did you say your name was?
- Where have you been all my life?
- Haven't we met somewhere before?
- What's a nice girl like you doing in a place like this?
- What's love got to do with it?
- Your place or mine?

96

BUDDHA PESTS

THEY'RE MANTRA-CHANTING, flower-peddling metaphysical mealybugs seeking help in the wrong direction, and you don't need to consult a spirit guide or the I Ching to spot them.

Avoiding them is something else. Difficult.

Usually dressed as if they've just come from a toga party, with shaved heads and Taras Bulba ponytails, these pseudo Dharma bums' only hygiene practice is brainwashing. They congregate at airports, bus terminals, train stations, rock concerts—wherever the most people can be annoyed—and panhandle persistently enough in the name of peace to give nonviolence a bad name.

If cornered by these Buddha pests, you can either follow the path of least resistance and surrender a quarter—or surrender to your natural instincts and swat 'em!

▲

97
WHAT YOU
SHOULD BELIEVE

THE WORD "SHOULD" is a New Age etymological pariah. Using it in public or private (in simple or compound sentences) is about as acceptable as a rabbi eating pork on Yom Kippur.

Considered by virtually all therapists, metaphysicians, and pilgrims on the path to life-acing enlightenment to be the most negative, guilt-inducing, self-destructive obscenity in the English language, "should" has been overwhelmingly voted the auxiliary verb most likely to be exorcised before the millennium.

Nonetheless, there are still some things that you *should* believe. And, at the risk of being lynched by my own silver cord, I've listed them below.

You should believe that:

- Taking a bath with a toaster is dangerous.
- Breathing is most beneficial when done on a daily basis.
- Bears relieve themselves in the woods.
- There's more to "self-discovery" than masturbation.
- Tomorrow is only a day away.
- Madonna isn't one.
- Jesus used to be Jewish.
- The earth is round.
- Unfoldment has nothing to do with sorting laundry.

98

How to Survive the Millennium

EVERY THOUSAND YEARS is a millennium and a New Age, and every thousand years there are thousands who feel they need more time to prepare for it.

How much more time do they need?

It's not like the universe is pulling a fast one. Millenniums have rolled around before. Regularly. And, quite frankly, they're no big deal.

If you want to make it through the year 2000, all you have to do is everything the Surgeon General tells you to—and, of course, pack up your troubles in your old kit bag and SMILE, SMILE, SMILE!

99

WHAT THE UNIVERSE DOES NOT PROVIDE

THE UNIVERSE IS your friend. Your best friend. Trust it, and it will provide you with *everything you need*—sometimes things you never knew you needed. Or even wanted.

But, as benevolent and giving as it is, there are still a few things in life that the universe does *not* provide.

Things the Universe Does Not Provide

- Daily TV listings
- Self-washing windows
- S.A.T. answers
- Low interest rates
- Jumper cables
- Room service
- Unlimited warranties on major appliances
- Wrinkle-free prunes
- Clean underwear

100

PARTING THOUGHTS

- After all is said and done, it usually is.

- Always think twice about something you can do only once.

- The quickest way to unleash powers you didn't know you had is to buy a Doberman.

- To achieve a real sense of your own worth, reconcile your bank statements monthly.

- Telepathy is just minding someone else's business.

- What's always disappointing about *déjà vu* is that you've seen it before.

- Everyone has had at least one out-of-body experience: *birth*.

- The upside of death is that it's a once-in-a-lifetime experience.

- The only sure way to avoid reincarnation is to stay alive.

101

IS THERE LIFE AFTER SHIRLEY?

WHO CARES? There's always *Time*.